THE GIRLS' GUIDE TO BUILDING A MILLION-DOLLAR BUSINESS

THE GIRLS' GUIDE TO BUILDING A MILLION-DOLLAR BUSINESS

Susan Wilson Solovic

AMACOM AMERICAN MANAGEMENT ASSOCIATION

New York ➤ Atlanta ➤ Brussels ➤ Chicago ➤ Mexico City ➤ San Francisco
Shanghai ➤ Tokyo ➤ Toronto ➤ Washington, D. C.

This publication is designed to provide accurate and authoritative information in
regard to the subject matter covered. It is sold with the understanding that the publisher is not engaged in rendering legal, accounting, or other professional service. If
legal advice or other expert assistance is required, the services of a competent professional person should be sought.

Library of Congress Cataloging-in-Publication Data

Solovic, Susan Wilson.
Girls' guide to building a million-dollar business / Susan Wilson Solovic.
    p. cm.
Includes index.
ISBN 978-0-8144-7419-8
1. Businesswomen. 2. Women-owned business enterprises. 3. New business enter-
prises. 4. Success in business. I. Title.
HD6072.5.S65 2007
658.1'1082—dc22

                                                                    2007027310

Printing number
10 9 8 7 6 5 4 3 2 1

To my wonderful father, Ray Wilson—
I am the luckiest girl in the world.

. And to my granddaughters,
Emma and Claire Solovic—
I hope someday you are million-dollar girls.

CONTENTS

FOREWORD

Isn't it wonderful when something you've been given not only meets more than your expectations, but greets you like an old friend whose eyes are on fire because her life has taken a great turn, and she wants to share it with you, because, after all, you are her great friend? That is the experience I had when reading Susan Solovic's wonderful new book, the book you now hold between your hopeful hands.

The subject of women in business is a dear one to me. For the past thirty years, I have worked closely with thousands of women, all of whom started their own business with hope and trepidation and the slight dizziness that takes over when you enter a strange new world. Mainly, though, my meeting with these women came after that first moment in which the lights were first turned on in their store, or their office, or their kitchen, or their once-used-as-a-bedroom-now-used-as-a-home-office area, with a sign on the door saying, this is mine, I just started it, oh, please, please be kind!

No, I met these same ladies not on the first day or before when I would have preferred to have met them to give them the benefit of all my years of experience, but years later. Some called two years later, some four, some eight, some more—when many of them had all but given up the ghost because they had finally come to that heart-deadening place where they simply couldn't figure out the answers to the multiple complex questions which were thrown their way:

Where does the money go at the end of the day? How come my favorite employee who I trusted with all of my heart simply decided not to come back one day, or the next, and didn't even bother to call? How come the banker who I thought was my friend doesn't answer my calls? Is that fair? Is that moral? Is that what a good banker does when you most need him? Do I deserve to feel hurt, to feel angry, to feel let down? Do I dare share this with anyone? Am I the only one who is feeling all these strange and sometimes oppressive feelings? Am I the only one feeling so distressed and depressed, knowing that I've got to get up tomorrow morning with a new face on and do it all again?

Well, fear not, ladies, Susan Solovic is here. And what a wonderful treat she's prepared for you all. No, you are not alone, Susan says. Let me count the ways. Yes, you are warriors, dear friends, as Susan will show you, and there is nothing more beautiful than a warrior facing down her fears when she doesn't know where her next buck is going to come from. Yes, all that is here, dear women warriors, dear ladies in business, and congratulations to you all. Read, take notice, and dig down deep where the well of strength in you is waiting. Because Susan Solovic is going to teach you how to grow.

Michael E. Gerber

PREFACE

As a writer and a journalist, I often find myself reporting on stories and topics about which I have no personal knowledge or experience. My job is to communicate to the best of my ability critical information so my audience can be well informed.

This book, however, is based not only on research and interviews, but also on my own personal experiences. As a cofounder and CEO of the new SBTV.com—small business television—I have been fortunate to help build a multimillion-dollar enterprise from the ground up. There have been thrilling moments, frustrating moments, and disheartening moments, but the journey has been incredible.

My goal is to show how you, too, can lead your enterprise to the million-dollar level, not only from my personal perspective but from the experience and insight of other women who have traveled this road. Because I am first and foremost a television journalist, I've interviewed many successful women entrepreneurs who will be weighing in on a variety of topics. I look forward to introducing you to my guests throughout the book. They are the real stars of the show.

ACKNOWLEDGMENTS

No one in this world is ever successful without great people who support, assist and believe in them. Certainly, I would not have been able to accomplish what I have done without wonderful friends, family, and business associates. I am blessed with a circle of support consisting of truly outstanding people, and I want to acknowledge them for all they have done:

First, there is my wonderful husband, George, who is my greatest fan. He believes in me and cheers me on. He's there to hold my hand when I need it and to kick me in the fanny when appropriate. He does everything in his power to help me succeed.

My two wonderful business partners, Michael Kelley and Dan Demko. I shall forever be indebted to you for believing in my dreams.

My team at SBTV.com, whose passion and vision inspire me everyday: Danita Blackwood, Lisa Constance, Meegan Jaycox, Patty Bausch, Steven Kelley, Nick Kubik, Chris Hanley, Patty Blancett, David Atkinson, Chris Golden, John Reichert, and Ramey Elliot.

The hundreds of outstanding women business leaders who have served as role models, confidantes, friends and sources of inspiration. There are far too many to mention, but I am thankful for all of you.

The many generous women who shared their time and insight with me as I was writing and researching this book. Your stories undoubtedly will encourage many other women to follow in your footsteps.

I am grateful for my treasured friends at my publisher, AMA-COM: Hank Kennedy, Kama Timbrell, Andy Ambraziejus, Irene Majuk, and last not but least, AMACOM's executive editor, Ellen Kadin, who took a chance with me six years ago, when AMACOM published my first book, *The Girls' Guide to Power and Success*. Thank you, Ellen, for everything.

INTRODUCTION

Congratulations. You have just opened the door to what hopefully will become one of the most exciting and rewarding journeys of your life: building a million-dollar business. Before you read on, take a minute to look at the front cover of this book. Notice the woman pictured there? Doesn't she look as though she's having the time of her life? Can't you hear her exclaim, "I did it!"? She has the world by the tail. That could be you.

This book is designed to help you reach that moment of sheer ecstasy. Not in an intimate sense, but the kind of ecstasy you feel from succeeding, from living your dreams, from being the person you were meant to be. As you read and learn tips and strategies outlined throughout the book, I want you to stay focused on that feeling. You deserve to feel empowered, energized, and wonderful every day of your life.

It's Your Turn to Be in the Spotlight

No matter what stage of life you are in at this point—please listen to me. It's time for you. There are far too many women who postpone or give up their personal dreams in order to take care of others in their lives. Obligations fill their days and their own passions get buried. Their personal identities are tied up in other people's lives.

As you read, I hope you'll learn how exhilarating sitting at the helm of a million-dollar enterprise can be—not only from the sense of personal accomplishment, but also from your ability to impact the world. As a million-dollar business owner, you can provide for your family, your employees, and their families. Through charitable contributions you can help others in need. Your leadership position in the business world empowers you with a voice that can make a difference in our government. And as a role model, you can touch thousands of others and inspire them to do great things with their lives. It doesn't get much better than that.

Join Millions of Women Who Get It

In 2006, the Center for Women's Business Research reported that there are 10.4 million privately held firms in the United States that are 50 percent or more owned by a woman. This statistic doesn't include companies such as mine, where I am the largest individual stockholder and the CEO, but I don't own 50 percent. So the actual number of women-owned and women-led businesses is much higher than what is officially recognized.

"Women are catching up to men across the world," says I. Elaine Allen, professor of statistics and entrepreneurship at Babson College in Massachusetts. Professor Allen was part of the Global Entrepreneurship Monitor (GEM) *2005 Report on Women and Entrepreneurship*. This research is part of the world's largest and longest-standing study of entrepreneurial activity, and it is the first comprehensive and timely study of women entrepreneurs around the globe.

Women are opening businesses at twice the rate of their male counterparts. It's the fastest growing segment of the U.S. economy. Women view business ownership as an opportunity for independence, creative control, and financial freedom. So the number of women jumping into the entrepreneurial pond isn't the issue. The issue is their ability to turn these businesses into large, sustainable, business operations.

"But maybe most women just don't want to grow their businesses?" is a response I often get to that statement. Sure, some women may not want to grow their businesses, and that's fine. However, are they really making that decision based on a true understanding of what is possible? I don't think they are.

Additionally, research from the Center of Women's Business Ownership notes nine out of ten women business owners want to expand their businesses and four in ten want their businesses to become as large as possible.

So we know the number of women-owned firms is exploding, and we also know that many want to grow and expand their business. The astounding statistic that drove me to write this book is the fact that fewer than 3 percent of women-owned businesses in the U.S. gross a million dollars or more in revenue. To increase that number, women need a guide to help them navigate the challenges of business ownership—hence *The Girls' Guide to Building a Million-Dollar Business*.

Inspiration for Success: What's Your Motivation?

Because you are reading this book, I know you are inspired to build a million-dollar business. That's important because successful women entrepreneurs are driven. They are ambitious, tenacious, and goal oriented. They are visionaries, innovators, and inventors.

As you start to grow your company, it's a good idea to step back and evaluate your motivation. According to Sharon Hadary, executive director of the Center for Women's Business Research:

> Our research shows that the first and foremost motivation for women to start their own business is the attraction of an entrepreneurial idea, where women see a new product or service that nobody is providing, and they would like to provide it. Or

they look at what they are doing for their current employer, and they believe they can do it just as well if not better and in a way to create economic independence for themselves.

For example, Valerie Freeman, CEO and founder of Imprimis Group, was on the faculty of a community college in Dallas, Texas, when word-processing technology appeared on the scene. Intuitively, she recognized this new technology would sweep the business world.

"Everyone was scared to death of it, but I thought it was wonderful, and I knew it was going to take over businesses in the future. So I decided to start a business to train, place, and consult in this newly emerging technology area," she says. Freeman has used the ever-changing nature of technology to grow her business over the last twenty-five years. Today, Imprimis boasts revenues of approximately $30 million with more than 1,500 professionals employed at client firms across the country.

Leaving a job at a major magazine publisher, where she enjoyed bankers' hours and a generous expense account, Dany Levy took a leap of faith because she was drawn to the immediacy of publishing on the Internet instead of the typical six-months lead times of print publishing. At first, she admits she questioned her sanity, but soon she realized she could use her skills and talents in publishing in a completely new way. Now she runs DailyCandy.com, a website devoted to the latest trends in fashion and fun, with over four million registered subscribers.

Taryn Rose used her knowledge and medical training as an orthopedic surgeon to create the ultimate luxury for busy women everywhere—a line of footwear that's both fashionable and comfortable. Her company, Taryn Rose International, now boasts annual sales of more than $30 million.

Former deputy administrator of the U.S. Small Business Administration, Melanie Sabelhaus, started out in the corporate world but identified a niche that would make her a very successful entrepreneur. While still holding her corporate post at IBM, she realized there was no suitable temporary corporate housing when she and her family were relocated to New York. "The Plaza Hotel was great, but not for a family of four, a nanny, and a live-in mother-in-law," she quips.

Sabelhaus experienced the same situation when she and her family were again moved to Baltimore. Once they were settled with a home of their own, she decided to test-market her idea of a fully-furnished "Corporate Executive Suite" by utilizing her own guest house. The idea took off almost immediately, and from there, Exclusive Interim Properties (EIP) was born.

Entrepreneurial women often see opportunities in new areas which are complete departures from their career experience or education. In 1988, with a good idea and grand plans, Patty Phillips left a successful commercial real estate career and opened Patty's Gourmet Pizza, a take-and-bake pizza business.

"I realized that people were dining in more, but did not have time to cook. My friends thought I was crazy for leaving a successful real estate career to start a company that sold unbaked pizzas. They said, 'But, Patty, you don't cook.' So I'd say, 'The pizzas are unbaked.' I'm glad to have proven them wrong, as we are doing very well," Phillips says. In addition to her original business, Phillips has added a wholesale company, which sells pizzas to hotels, restaurants, and other companies in the hospitality industry.

Independence and control over the final product or outcome attracts some women to business ownership. "Many women feel they had no opportunity to influence the direction of the business. It wasn't that they didn't get promoted. The issue was not being able to influence the organization in a strategic way," explains Sharon Hadary.

Having joined a local independent temp agency, Bonny Filandrinos helped to grow the business from a start-up operation with minimal revenues to a fairly successful company in only five years. "I was responsible for bringing in all the revenues, but I became frustrated because I had no say in how resources were put to use. I had the urge to get the heck out of there and start my own company. If I was going to have all the responsibility, I'd rather do it myself," she says. Today, she is president of her own company, Staffing Solutions, which generates more than $3 million in annual revenue.

The desire to create a flexible work environment is also a significant motivator. Corporate careers typically fail to adapt to the nuances of women's lives. With the aid of today's sophisticated technology, you can start and build a business from anywhere at any time. It's possible to run a global company from your garage, allowing your work schedule to accommodate your life schedule.

"This isn't about women versus men. The reality for women, especially women with children, is cultural: women are still the primary caretakers of children—and now, aging parents," wrote Alicia Rodriquez in response to a *Businessweek.com* article entitled "Women Leading the Way in Startups" (May 17, 2006).

Expressing a similar sentiment, Margaret Heffernan of FastCompany.com wrote, "Some 420 women a day start new businesses. They do so because they're sick of being forced into male paradigms. They're sick of being patronized. They're sick of being powerless. And they know they're good" (May 24, 2006).

Sharon Hadary is quick to point out it's not that women are looking to work fewer hours, but that they want to manage their time better. "Being able to go to a child's school play, or being able to spend time with ill parents, or whatever. It isn't that women are working fewer hours, it's that they have flexibility when they own their own businesses."

Women business owners are creating cultures with a family-friendly environment. "There is one woman in particular I am aware of, who runs a business with about 200 to 300 employees, and generates about $15 million," Hadary notes. "We were sitting in her conference room talking, and suddenly I realized there were about four children playing under the conference table. I asked the woman about the children, and she explained there was a school holiday that day, and she had a choice. 'I can tell people they can't bring their children to work, and people will take the day off,' she said. 'Or I can tell them to bring the children in, and I'll get a full day contributing to the business.'"

Hadary adds, "So I think what women are doing is not only personal but also for their employees, by creating a culture of flexibility that allows women to fulfill both their personal and professional goals."

Make Way for the Million-Dollar Mompreneurs

There are a variety of paths that lead to a million-dollar-plus business. One that might seem unlikely at first is really one of the segments that is booming: million-dollar *Mompreneurs.*® These are women with children who are starting businesses from their homes in order to earn additional income and provide a better quality of life for their families.

According to Mom Inventors, Inc., there are 82 million moms in the United States. They represent the largest source of untapped entrepreneurial intelligence in the country. Mom Inventors produces products made by and for moms that are sold through retailers nationwide. Each product carries the "Mom Invented" brand, which symbolizes the dynamic creativity of moms everywhere.

Mompreneurs are getting in on the franchising craze too. Founded in 2000 by California mom Brenda Dronkers, Pump It Up offers families and kids an indoor private party facility with huge interactive inflatables to climb and play on. Dronkers started the company to be able to stay at home with her kids and to have flexibility in her schedule. In 2002, she added partner Terry Dillenburg, and they began franchising. Today the company has grown to $53 million in annual revenues.

Olivia Mullin of Brentwood, Tennessee, was called by the lure of entrepreneurism after the birth of her first child. She made the decision to be a stay-at-home mom, taking a break from her career as a registered nurse and organ-donation coordinator. It was then she taught herself calligraphy and started offering her services to local paper stores. Initially, she addressed wedding invitations but soon began creating personalized stationery and gifts. The business took off, and today her products can be found in forty-five retail outlets across the country.

Drawing on her pre-motherhood experience in the fitness world, Lisa Druxman, founder and CEO of Stroller Strides, not only created a business for herself, but was able to help other moms in the process. She came up with a concept to help get back into shape after pregnancy. Stroller Strides offers total fitness programs for new moms that they can do while pushing their baby strollers. She also offers franchise opportunities for other would-be mompreneurs throughout the United States, as well as several locations in Canada and her newest location in Okinawa, Japan.

The Challenges Ahead

There is much to celebrate when it comes to the progress women entrepreneurs have made, as outlined in a brief historical perspective in the Appendix. However, there's still much work to be done in a number of areas to make it easier for women to compete and succeed. As I said in my first book, *The Girls' Guide to Power and Success,* women have self-sabotaging beliefs that limit their ability to grow their businesses. There are also systemic obstacles, such as lack of access to capital, to markets, and to technical assistance, as well as a lack of credibility. None of these challenges are insurmountable if you know how to deal with them.

That being said, the one issue I find the most problematic is the lack of credibility women business owners face. This is an issue that affects every aspect of business operations. When you aren't taken seriously it is more difficult to land big contracts and increase your sales. It also limits your ability to obtain financing to expand your business operations.

Women who run successful businesses are sometimes seen as what is known as a front—someone whose title may be CEO, but who really isn't involved in the operations of the business. It's sad but true. This gender bias is experienced by many of us who run large companies. I think it's unfortunate, yet oddly funny when my husband and I are introduced to someone at a social gathering. The conversation usually turns to him and the question is asked, "So what do you do?" In fact, one woman went so far as to say, "What do you do? Work to support her?"

Theresa Alfaro Daytner is a serial entrepreneur who currently owns Daytner Construction Group, a construction project management and consulting firm. "It makes my husband nuts that people still perceive that he set me up in this business to get certified as a woman-owned firm. Where appropriate and when we get a chance, we set people straight. Some people will always choose to see what they think. . . . and others are pleasantly surprised that I'm an actual entrepreneur," she says.

If you already own your own business, you may have found yourself in business settings where you have been mistaken for the secretary, while a male employee is assumed to be the authority figure. Margery Kraus is president and CEO of APCO Worldwide, a global public relations firm that works with major corporations and governments to build public private partnerships to solve societal problems. Her firm employs many high-powered men in her firm, including former executives and members of Congress. When she and her predominately male team attend introductory meeting with potential clients, she is often ignored until the prospects come to the realization that she is the CEO.

"They always assume it's the men in the room who are running the show. But, you know, at this point I love being underestimated because it is a real competitive advantage," Kraus says.

Texas entrepreneur Billie Bryant took over the reigns of her company CESCO, Inc., an office equipment sales and service company, when her husband was diagnosed with a very serious heart condition. The transition was difficult because she wasn't taken seriously. As Bryant says:

> I was shocked by what I experienced. I was a woman who had been active in the neighborhood. I had held leadership positions in the PTA, church, and civic organizations. I really thought that the same atmosphere would transition into the business world, but I found there was very little understanding of the woman business owner or the fact that I was capable of competing.

Believe it or not, it's not just the men who want to discount you. For example, Allison Evanow recently started her business, Square One Organic Vodka, and is working toward the goal of reaching $1 million. Allison spent ten years in middle and executive-level management in wines and spirits marketing and is a seasoned vet in the market. But she is amazed to hear other people's perceptions of her business now that she's on her own. According to Evanow:

> I hate to say it, but in some instances when I have spoken to other women who are not business women about my business, I have often gotten the comment, "You mean you actually STARTED the company yourself? But it's really you and your husband, isn't it?" I have been shocked at how many non-business women have automatically assumed there was a man involved, or behind the scenes, and don't really believe we are doing something "big" until they hear we are getting written up in *Oprah* or *Bon Appetit* or some other big magazine that validates us.

The moral of these stories is to go in with your eyes wide open and don't let perceptions or challenges stall your efforts. It's not a level playing field for women, but you'll find lots of examples throughout this book of how you can successfully deal with gender bias and other business challenges.

Changing the Paradigm: Resources for Next Steps

In Chapter 10 of this book, you'll find a list of great resources that can help you with next steps for business growth. One of those resources is a nonprofit organization called Count Me In. Founded by Nell Merlino, Count Me In is an online microlender that provides loans to women to help them get their businesses started. Merlino believes women's financial independence is the missing piece in the evolution of equal rights for women.

In 2004, Merlino's organization, in conjunction with OPEN from American Express, launched a program called Make Mine a $Million Business.

The goal of Make Mine a $Million Business is to help one million women entrepreneurs reach $1 million in revenue by the year 2010. According to information recently released by Count Me In, if one million women were to set their sights on achieving $1 million in annual revenue by 2010, they would add up to $700 billion in productivity to the U.S. economy and add as many as four million new jobs. During the October 2006 "Make Mine a $Million Business" program, Senator Hillary Rodham Clinton, a proponent of women's business issues, addressed the packed house on the importance of women-owned businesses to the economy, saying, "Women in previous generations walked a long and hard road to get to where we are today." Then, after referring to the small number of women-owned companies that have crossed the million-dollar threshold, she went on to say, "That means there's a lot of room for improvement. Women are not yet fulfilling their potential in the economy, in the marketplace—not yet pushing the limits of what women-owned businesses can achieve."

Hitting the Million-Dollar Mark

There are obstacles you'll encounter on your million-dollar journey, but you can and hopefully will overcome them as you build your company. This book is divided into three parts. Part I is designed to help you to personally lay the ground work to build a wildly successful business. Part II walks you through the tactical issues of building a million-dollar business as well as provides some great tips and advice to help you build your business growth. Part III provides strategic options for your business model that can help accelerate your company's growth.

It's your time and your turn. Be among the ranks of women who are changing the world and who are living the lives they so justly deserve. This book will give you the tools, the insight, and the resources you need. The rest is up to you. I'll be cheering you on.

PART ONE

Laying the Groundwork for
a Million-Dollar Business

LAYING THE GROUNDWORK for business expansion is like laying the foundation of a house. Without it you can't build the house. Likewise, without a solid base for your business you can't build a million-dollar enterprise.

1

START THE MILLION-DOLLAR JOURNEY

You Look Like a Million

What does a million-dollar woman business owner look like? What type of woman runs a million-dollar enterprise? How would you describe her? Does Meryl Streep's character in *The Devil Wears Prada* come to mind? Do you envision a glamorous woman dressed in Chanel, wearing Manolo Blahnik shoes with a Prada bag, dripping in Tiffany diamonds and stepping out of an expensive foreign car barking orders at everyone? If that's what you think, think again.

If you want to know what a million-dollar woman business owner looks like—look in the mirror. That's right, she looks just like you. She could be you. She could also be your sister, your next-door neighbor, your college roommate or sorority sister, even your daughter. You may have bumped into her in the grocery line, at soccer practice, dance recital or PTA meeting. Million-dollar women business owners come in all shapes, sizes, ages and from all walks of life. Rarely is a woman business owner a glam queen, or diva. While you might see her wearing Chanel, it could easily be from the local consignment shop. But she could also be wearing jeans and a T-shirt with a hard hat and boots.

As for her preferred mode of transportation, successful business mavens drive everything from Ford trucks to moving vans to airplanes. You probably won't hear her barking orders, either. I have found most successful women entrepreneurs are compassionate and passionate. They sincerely care about the health of their businesses, their employees and their communities.

Revealing a Well-Kept Secret: Knowing Where to Look

Surprised to learn how seemingly ordinary million-dollar women business owners can be? You aren't alone. The incredible stories of these amazing women are one of the world's best kept secrets. Typically, women entrepreneurs don't flaunt their success because that's not their style. If you have ever read any of the gender communication books, you know men do a much better job of spotlighting their accomplishments than women do. (If you'd like to learn more about these differences, I recommend my first book *The Girls' Guide to Power and Success.*) Couple that with inherent gender bias and a lack of credibility women business owners face, and you have an unrecognized group of inspiring, successful women.

Why is this important for you to know? Well, in order to build your own million-dollar business, you should get to know some of these fabulous women so you don't feel as though you are headed down an unbeaten path. There is comfort in knowing many trailblazing women have forged the way. An important first step for you on your journey to building a million-dollar business is to be able to visualize yourself running a multimillion-dollar enterprise. However, it's tough to visualize something you've never seen before. My job is to reveal the secret of where you'll find these incredible women business leaders.

Unfortunately, the general media is not the answer. Mainstream media only portrays two types of women in business: those who have small, micro-businesses, and the entrepreneurial divas, such as Oprah or Martha Stewart. The rest of us might as well be chopped liver.

"Say 'entrepreneurial woman' to the press and their eyes glaze over. It could be the most unique thing you've ever heard, but if you say it's a woman it's going to get ignored. It makes you want to pitch the story and leave out the fact it's a woman until the very last minute," says Cheryl Womack, who is currently the CEO of five companies and also serves as the chairwoman of Leading Women Entrepreneurs of the World.™ Womack founded VCW Inc., an insurance agency designed to serve independent contractor truck drivers. Within twenty years, she started four other companies with combined annual revenues of $100 million. Then she sold them all in 2002, and established her current list of companies, which include an accounting and tax planning firm (VCW Accounting Services LLC), a charter jet operation (Just Jets Inc.), and a real estate company (R&A Properties LLC).

"The media profiles the monster mega businesses. So if you are a little bitty business, the only thing you can look at to compare yourself with in the papers is a monster mega business. So the message that is being sent is either you are going to be a little one-armed basket-weaving business, or you've got to be the superstar. But there is so much in between," Womack adds.

Images of successful women business owners in the media are usually less than flattering. That's why I asked you about what type of woman you envision running a million-dollar business. Think about the successful business women you see in the movies or in television programs. Isn't she usually the villain or a hard-core vixen? She is portrayed as the quintessential "B."

Taking it one step further, women get significantly less press coverage as authority figures, period. That makes it all the more difficult for our society to view women as experts and business leaders.

Women in Communications conducted a study a few years ago and found only 5 percent of the stories on the front page of newspapers were about or written by a woman, and fewer than 10 percent of stories inside the newspaper were about or by women.

As president and founder of the Women Presidents' Organization (WPO), Marsha Firestone works to promote media recognition of the women who belong to her organization. Criteria for membership in the WPO includes over one million dollars in revenue for a service business and over two million dollars for a product business. Most of its members have significantly larger businesses than the threshold requirements. In fact, the average revenues of the group are $12 million, the average number of employees is 89, and the average number of years in business is 21. It goes without saying that women who belong to the WPO are among the best of the best.

"One February I was preparing to go to the WPO conference in San Francisco, where we had 415 attendees. There was a section in the *New York Times* on small business. It was a ten page section. There was not a single mention of a woman-owned business. Not even one of the authors was a female," Firestone stated.

Firestone wrote twice to the editors of the *New York Times* and was never acknowledged in any way. "There was not one word from the *Times*. So I find that the regular media really doesn't pay much attention to us and do not take us very seriously."

There's no doubt the media needs to be better informed. But in the meantime, where do you turn to learn more about women entrepreneurs?

First, look for publications that focus on women business leaders. These types of periodicals can inspire and educate you about growing your business. One such publication is *Enterprising Women*, whose publisher, Monica Smiley, says, "We give these invisible women business owners a voice. Our publication is already being used to mentor women, and I think it is important not just to have the stories about the ones that are celebrities, but the real people who go out there and work very hard and make a success out of it but don't have a household name."

"The readers of *Enterprising Women* magazine really have the opportunity to focus in on role models. They get to see people who look like them and who have had the same set of experiences they have had in treading the waters of starting, running, and growing success-ful enterprises," adds Susan Bari, president emeritus and founding architect of WBENC—Women's Business Enterprise National Council—and now president of a new company, Fly Fast, LLC.

The Internet is also a great source of knowledge, and regardless of where you are located you can connect into the community of women business owners. Spend time on the various search engines looking for information about women business owners. There are numerous web-sites designed to assist women who are building business enterprises. You'll also discover great success stories along with tips, tools, and resources. I have included a number of them in the Great Resources section of this book. In addition, there are also social networking sites which provide an excellent way to connect with other women business owners and learn from their experiences. For example, at SBTV.com we offer business owners an opportunity to join discussion groups about specific topics of interest. There are also mentor-led forums. Plus, you can upload your own video, audio and text to showcase your business. Finally, our small business community provides for great networking opportunities and resources. So if you are looking for assistance in growing your marketing firm, you can ask and learn online. You may even be able to find a mentor who can help guide you.

Another smart strategy is getting actively involved in some of the women-business-owner membership organizations—not only at the local chapter level, but at the national level too. When I was getting my business off the ground, I attended national conferences and accepted leadership roles with several of the organizations. Through these groups I met so many women who absolutely blew me away and encouraged me every step of the way.

The real turning point for me was in 1999 when Marsha Firestone of the WPO gave me the opportunity to start a St. Louis Chapter of the Women Presidents' Organization. Having recently started my own business, I was struggling. The WPO paid its local facilitators about $500 a month back then, which for me wasn't bad, but the real value was getting to know the women presidents. At first I was intimidated about calling them and inviting them to join the chapter. But soon I learned how warm and welcoming they were. And I certainly learned a tremendous amount from them just by listening to their business stories and challenges during our monthly meetings. Even though I was only the facilitator, they began to include me in the group and ask me about my business. Wow! It was like having a room filled with the most expensive business consultants anyone could afford. Their insight and guidance was priceless.

I continued to lead the chapter until I became a member myself in 2005. It reminded me of a graduation ceremony. Officially, I had graduated and was now one of them: a million-dollar woman business owner.

You'll benefit tremendously from the experiences and viewpoints of other women who have walked down this path. But you must take the initiative to discover them. Once you do, you'll be inspired and better equipped to pursue your business dreams.

If You Don't Believe in You, No One Else Can

What's fun in life is knowing you're not good at something and then making yourself good at it.

—Lesley Stahl

The only way you'll ever cross the million-dollar threshold with your business is to believe in yourself. There's no way around it. If you are someone whose confidence waxes and wanes, you'll find your million-dollar journey more difficult if not impossible. You should know exactly what you are capable of doing and what your abilities are. You must be grounded in those beliefs and be able to hold onto them when things don't turn out the way you expected. You more than anyone else need to believe in your ability to succeed. "Self-doubt is one of the main reasons business owners don't achieve the level of success they could," says Dr. Rachna Jain, a Baltimore psychologist and business coach.[1]

So before your journey gets underway, stop and recognize how truly amazing you are. Focus on all the positives in your life. Really take time to get reacquainted with yourself. What are your strengths? What are your passions? What is special and unique about you? What are your core competencies?

Why is getting to know yourself so important? Because as a business owner your judgments, decisions, strategies, and ideas will be repeatedly questioned. When you make a good decision, you get to take the credit. When you make a bad decision, you get the blame. It's all on your shoulders. You need to be able to trust your instincts and abilities without constantly second guessing yourself. You should be able to cut through the garbage. That's not always an easy thing to do. Throughout our lives people place labels on us, and those labels—right or wrong—become part of who we are. For example, someone may have told you as a child that you are a poor speller. So a tiny internal voice regularly reminds you that you are poor speller. Interestingly, whether or not you really are a poor speller, you may have become a poor speller over time. It's a self-fulfilling prophecy.

When I was entering the seventh grade, the principal of the middle school used our recent scores on a standardized test to determine class placement. I was never good at taking standardized tests. My scores ranged from very high to pretty darn low. As luck would have it, my score in the sixth grade fell on the pretty darn low side. So even though my grades were excellent, the principal put me in the class for mentally challenged students while all my friends were in the accelerated class.

My mother promptly paid a visit to the school principal, who told her the most she could hope for me would be a vocational education. My perception of myself changed. I quit trying. I figured what's the point in trying when you are mentally challenged? I didn't get back on track until my sophomore year in high school when a school counselor encouraged me to aim for the top of my class. Thankfully, I listened and I graduated fourth in my class. Labels are powerful and can be damaging. Even today, I struggle with those early images of myself.

Sociologist Charles Horton Cooley developed a theory he called the "Looking-Glass Self." Simply stated, the theory propagates the belief that the sense of self is the product of our social interactions with others. The theory describes three states: First, we imagine how we present ourselves to others. Then, we determine how others evaluate us. And finally, we develop a feeling about ourselves as a result of these impressions. Our self-image, self-worth, and self-esteem are derived from the way we perceive others see us.

You must have a clear sense of your true self in order to visualize yourself leading a multimillion-dollar enterprise. Whether you think you can or you think you can't—you are right. Your mindset and your perceptions of yourself are integral to your success. When you peel away the layers of the onion and take a good look at yourself, you might be surprised to discover hidden dreams, talents and skills. Maybe you've been afraid to push forward with your business venture because you have accepted someone else's perception of you. Maybe you've been told you aren't good at managing people or reading financial statements. Is that really true? Maybe you just need a little training or support, or maybe you need to reach out and find the resources to augment your skill set.

During a entrepreneurship seminar I taught, a woman in the group asked for advice about growing her ten-year-old business.

Despite an innovative product and several solid commercial accounts, she struggled to keep the doors open year after year. Through a series of questions, I explored challenges that were holding her back. The class and I tried to help her envision new strategies and markets, but we ran into dead-ends. However, throughout our discussion there was one constant issue—or person—that kept cropping up, her husband. Apparently, he consistently told her she couldn't do one thing or another, and she believed it. Even though we all tried to convince her otherwise, she couldn't let go, and as a result her self-esteem and confidence were low. If she couldn't believe in herself, no one else could either.

"Some of the best advice I could offer someone who wants to grow their business is to develop confidence, particularly because most women business leaders don't see themselves as strongly as they should. For me, getting my MBA was a wonderful thing because it gave me a credential that many people don't have. It's probably symbolic, but I think it shows you are qualified and helps give you confidence and helps others see you in a stronger light," says Ann Drake, CEO of DSC Logistics, a leading supply-chain management company with a nationwide network consisting of 30 locations. The company focuses on supply-chain solutions and capabilities that are adaptable, versatile, and based on changing customer needs.

Building a million-dollar business requires confidence and strong sense of self. Don't let old perceptions and labels stand in your way of building your dream. Most importantly, don't let someone else's negative opinion or idea of what you should or shouldn't be doing stand in your way. Make your own evaluations and judgments. Listen to feedback, but evaluate it carefully. Remember, just because someone says something about you doesn't make it true. Listen with a secret resolve that you know something they don't know. You know what great things you can accomplish so just smile and get started—make it happen.

You've Seen and Conquered Before

Take the chances necessary to achieve your dreams. My mother always told me, "Leap and the net will appear."
—Tamara Monosoff, founder and CEO of Mom Inventors

So far I've talked about the importance of tapping into the community of successful women business owners and believing in yourself and your abilities so you can visualize yourself as a million-dollar business owner. Hopefully, you are nodding your head in agreement at this point.

Now, I want to help you understand how to shore up your confidence level to take action and make it happen. During your journey there will be times when you face challenges or risks that cause your knees to shake and your palms to sweat profusely. Your self-doubt may creep to the surface and you consider throwing in the towel. "What was I thinking?" you ask.

Before you turn and run, stop and think about all the times you've been in tough situations and you've been able to figure it out. Even though I've never met you, I am certain you have successfully faced challenges in your life. All of us have. Somewhere along the way, either personally or professionally, we've all had to face difficult situations. Hopefully, regardless of the outcome you learned from those situations, and most importantly you survived. Keep telling yourself, I've seen and conquered before. That's what million-dollar women business owners do. They draw upon their past experiences and successes to help them as they tackle new challenges. They know they are smart enough to figure it out. Just ask yourself—what's the worst thing that could happen.

If you ask that question, and the answer is that the worst that can happen is acceptable, go for it. That doesn't mean you'll be right all the time. Trust me, I've made lots of mistakes. But no mistake ever put me out of business or was so destructive that the business couldn't move forward. If you don't stop and consider it from this perspective you may act too conservatively and not grow.

As WPO founder Marsha Firestone says, "Your total life experience is like a graduate school in life. You have all your job-related experiences, and if you are involved in nonprofit you take leadership roles, and that, too, gives you the confidence to continue. It's that experience that validates you."

While working in a doctor's office, Loreley Fortin decided to start a specialty advertising products company, Daystar Promotions. Initially, she ran the business on the side as a part-time effort to supplement her income. But as the business grew her boss gave her an ultimatum—her job or the business. She says:

> I was scared to death to let go of that weekly paycheck, but I chose the business. Obstacles that come into your life are just roadblocks. They are just fears that you have to overcome. I just asked myself, "What would happen if I didn't do this? What's the worst thing that could happen?" For me the worst thing that could happen was that I would have to go out and get another job. But when I asked myself if I *didn't* do this, and I was sixty years old and looking back at my life, it would have been worse to not have tried.

Another successful entrepreneur, Julia Rhodes, president and founder of Kleenslate Concepts, an international product development company, mirrors Fortin's feelings. "One of my biggest obstacles was fear. Fear of the unknown. I had a secure job. I had a paycheck coming in every month and health benefits. I was paying down my house and the next thing I knew, I'd given all that up, taken my retirement, refinanced my house, and I was leaping into this pragmatic world of business," she says.

Lisa Kable and Ann Buivid, cofounders of Artemis Woman, are two such women who drew upon their past experience and knowledge to give them the courage to spring from the corporate world and join the ranks of women entrepreneurs. The two met at Remington

Products Personal Care Division, a venture-backed turn-around. Buivid was the president and Kable was the marketing director.

"We got our inspiration to start Artemis Woman after spending too much time and energy convincing our board and CEO what women wanted in products. Imagine running a women's wellness business with a brand name Remington, which on a good day meant men's shavers, and on a bad day meant guns," says Kable.

The duo launched Artemis Woman in April 2002, and the company shipped its first product in the summer of 2003. Artemis Woman is a consumer products company which develops, markets, and sells home spa and beauty products to women through mass market retailers. Today, the company is a multimillion-dollar business with five full-time and three part-time employees.

Corporate experience gave the founders of Artemis Woman the confidence and experience they needed to start and grow their business, but many women are taking other paths to entrepreneurship. In fact, more and more young women are launching their own businesses at an early age.

Maggie Laughlin is a great example. At 23, an age when most young women are still trying to find their way in their professional lives, Laughlin launched Laughlin Promotions—a company that provides advertising specialty services to corporations, schools, sporting teams, and nonprofit organizations. "A lot of people tested me when I first started out. At my age, a lot of people were hesitant when I walked into their offices. The question always was, 'Is she going to be able to do this?' But they saw that I gave it my all, and I always came through for them," Laughlin recalls.[2]

That's why her sales grew 50 percent her second year in business. Since that time, the company has sustained a constant growth. Today, Laughlin manages a portfolio of nearly 500 clients and she is aggressively pursuing her goal of a $1 million sales year.

By the way, it's okay to feel a few butterflies in your stomach. That's different. In fact, nervous energy enhances your performance.

Ask any professional athlete or entertainer, and I am confident they'll tell you a lack of a little adrenal rush means a lackluster performance. I can personally vouch for that fact. The few times I didn't feel butterflies in my stomach before a speech or performance were the times when I didn't do my best.

Bonny Filandrinos says she was scared to death when she started her multimillion-dollar staffing services. "I literally suffered from panic and anxiety attacks every single day my first year. Some of the companies that I called on were companies that I had already done business with, so they knew me, but I was walking in with a different hat on and it was overwhelming for me. I learned I literally just had to deal with it," she says.

Most women will tell you as they were starting and growing their businesses they had moments where they questioned themselves. "What in the world am I doing?" Building a business is like being on a wild roller coaster ride. There are moments of excitement and there are moments of sheer terror, but at the end of the day it is a great ride. It is one of the most rewarding experiences you'll ever have.

Pamela Chambers O'Rourke left the corporate IT world to start her own company, ICON Information Consultants, because she knew she could do it better. But the fear didn't set in until after the fact:

> I got a one-room office. I had no clients. I had a database but no consultants, and on my second day I sat there and looked around and said, "What in the hell have I done?" I cried for a minute and then I said, "Wait a minute. This is not your personality. You're gonna get up and go and make one more dollar than you made at your last job." And I made $2.5 million my first year.

Whatever your age, whatever your experience, rely on your life experiences to shore up your confidence as you build your business.

Whenever you confront something scary—just stop and think about all the other times you've confronted challenges and you succeeded. You are smart. You are talented. You can do it. What's the worst that can happen?

Grit Your Teeth and Go for It

Determination is another key element of success. You might be surprised to learn that many great businesses have folded simply because of a lack of determination, and a lot of not-so-great businesses have succeeded because the owner was willing to do whatever it takes. Determination can make up for a lot of short-falls including capital, personnel, marketing and skills.

Million-dollar women business owners have an intense desire to succeed, and it's that desire combined with their passion, commitment, perseverance, and a lot of elbow grease that allows them to build successful enterprises. Most importantly, because they believe whole-heartedly in their businesses and their abilities, they are willing to do whatever it takes to ensure its success.

There's nothing glamorous about building a million-dollar enterprise. In fact, the early days are about as unglamorous as they can get. You make personal sacrifices and work long, hard hours. You sweep the floors, stuff envelopes, and drive your own delivery truck. One woman backed her delivery truck the wrong way down a one-way street in a major snow storm to make sure her product arrived on time. There's no room for a big ego, and you don't have time to sweat the small stuff. You dig in and get it done.

When Rebecca Boenigk and her mother, Jaye Congleton, started Neutral Posture, an ergonomic chair manufacturing company, the business was located in Boenigk's garage. The early days were lean, to say the least, but the mother-daughter team truly believed in their product, and so they didn't mind the modest surroundings and doing everything themselves. They took turns taking orders, and they worked together assembling the chairs and shipping them out. When the neighbors started complaining about the garage-based business, they moved into what they describe as "a terrible old building."

"It was a bigger space, but no more glamorous than a garage. We had one telephone and a 50-foot cord. We'd take it from the office to the production tables, and if the phone rang we'd stop what we were doing and answer the phone like in an office. I'd transfer them to Rebecca, and no one knew where we were," Congleton remembers.

When Dany Levy started DailyCandy.com, her business card read: #1 Christopher Street, Suite 8A. Her office was nothing more than her kitchen table in her Manhattan apartment. If you've ever been in a typical Manhattan apartment, you know how small that must have been. Despite the fact her business is all about trends and fashion, those early days included a lot of Ben and Jerry's ice cream and tuna from a can. Levy did everything herself, from buying the staples and toilet paper to making collection calls.

Shoe manufacturer Taryn Rose also remembers doing it all in the early days—everything from invoicing, to packing the boxes, to correcting manufacturing mistakes. Once she remembers having to replace every single insole in 500 pairs of shoes. But for Rose and most successful female entrepreneurs, acting as chief cook and bottle washer is a part of the process. It's the thrill of the journey that keeps you going.

Many women fail when they make the transition into business ownership because they aren't prepared for the lifestyle of a business start-up—particularly if they come from corporate America. If you work for someone else, do you ever wonder whether or not there is going to be toilet paper in the restroom? Probably not. But when you run your own business, if you don't buy it—it's not there. Being willing to push forward through anything and everything separates the winners from the wannabe's.

Based on my experience, the two greatest predictors of success are confidence and determination. If you are confident and determined, it matters little what industry you are in, where you live, how much money you have, or how much education you've acquired. Confidence creates the courage and strength to do what others only dream about. Determination provides the stamina to cross the finish line.

THINK BIG AND BOLD

THERE ARE THREE perceptions about successful women you absolutely need to dispel if you are going to become a million-dollar business success:

1. Ambitious women are selfish.

2. Women who want to make a lot of money are greedy.

3. Powerful women are bad.

False, false, false. All false. Society wires women's brains to think that making money, being ambitious, and becoming powerful is unfeminine. So you should re-wire your thinking. There's nothing wrong with being ambitious, making money and being powerful.

Shout It Out

Now that we've gotten that out of the way, repeat this sentence: *I deserve to be successful.*

Okay. Now muster the courage to announce your intentions to the world. Beat your chest and should it out. Write it down. Tell your best friend. Heck, tell everyone you know. Post a big sign on your bathroom mirror that reminds you every day that you are going to be a huge success. You'll never achieve success by passively and silently wishing and hoping for it. Today is the day. You have to ask for what you want in life and go out and make it happen. Dream the big dreams.

Some of you reading this book may just be starting your business, and others may already have established enterprises. The current status of your business isn't important. Thinking big and bold is what it's all about. It's important for women to have grand dreams. Why? Because too many of us are conditioned to think small, and we are afraid to think about creating major, multimillion-dollar enterprises.

Kristie Darien is the executive director of the Legislative Office for the National Association for the Self-Employed, or NASE. Kristie says, "Part of the problem is small business owners in general are, quite frankly, accustomed to being small. That is why taking that next step to grow their business can be daunting for micro-business owners."

The underlying difference between companies that start small and stay small and those that start small but get big is the attitude of the owner. Breaking out of the "small" mindset and thinking "big" is what most million-dollar business women say unleashed their potential.

Patty Phillips recalls her first business plan as being a perfect example of big, bold, and audacious. "I had no restaurant experience except three months as a waitress. But I decided I was going to have six stores in six months, create all these jobs for people who really needed them, and then make enough money to go travel the world and play polo," she admits. For the first two years she didn't have a day off, and to date she hasn't played polo. Perhaps that's because the founder of Patty's Presto Pizza, Inc. and Patty's Gourmet Take-and-Bake Pizza stores continues to think big. She has struck a deal with a Midwestern restaurant consultant and investor for an aggressive roll-out of the concept, where customers place an order and then bake the pie at home. Phillips said the business plan sets a goal of opening 500 locations in five years, which could make the company's rollout the largest of the year. Franchising deals that call for fifty restaurants a year are considered aggressive.

Survival was the name of the game when Mary Quigg and her husband started Vandover, which provides career management and relocation transition services worldwide. As Quigg explains:

> I was dreaming big from day one, because I saw a real need for support for relocating spouses in dual income families. We laughed about "big thinking" taking place on my own time AFTER meeting monthly overhead. Big thinking got stalled and sidetracked several times for lack of time and capital—but every chance I had I returned to my dream.

A bold public statement made Allison Evanow, founder of Square One Organic Vodka, realize she was ready to go for it. "For us, it was stating that we want to be at $10 million by 2010. That was the key statement. It was actually the setting of a goal of $10 million that was and is a great motivator."

WPO founder and president, Marsha Firestone, previously taught a start-up business course. At the beginning of the course, she asked the participants what their dream was. "I would say that 90 percent of them said, 'I just want to support myself' or 'I would enjoy some additional income.' But those who said, 'I want to have a great business . . . I want it to be global. I have to be a zillion-dollar business.'—those were the women who had the big dreams and who were the most motivated to succeed."

Successful women business owners have a vision about where they see their business going. They are clear about wanting to own a business of a substantial size. They are driven, and they are constantly out there pushing ahead to achieve their goals. Nothing is going to stand in the way of that vision. Women who successfully build multimillion-dollar enterprises aren't embarrassed or shy about sharing their vision with others.

Research supports this premise. According to the Center for Women's Business Research, the more goal-directed you are, the more likely you are to accelerate the growth of your company. Even in the face of adversity that desire doesn't dwindle.

Granted not everyone wants to run a major enterprise, and that's okay. But if you have a desire, a passion, to really build something— to create an entity that is bigger than you by yourself—then, embrace your dreams. Don't ignore them. Shout it from the rooftops. Let the world know to watch out because here you come.

Mind Over Money

Here is what we have to understand about your male counterparts. While we may fake orgasms, they fake finances.

—Suze Orman

Women and money is a subject I dislike writing about because I don't understand why women continue to have issues with money. When are women going to wake up to reality? What's wrong with making money? A friend of mine's daughter is a talented young lady in her late twenties who is dating a successful guy from an affluent family. "If I marry him, I'll never have to worry about money, and I won't have to work unless I want to," she said. I really don't get it.

Did you know the average age of widowhood in this country is about 57 years? Think about the divorce rates. Fifty percent or more of all marriages end in divorce. That number goes up if it's your second time around. If you aren't able to provide for yourself and your family, who do you expect will take care of you? Why don't women understand the importance of financial independence?

Financial independence means you have the control and wherewithal to make choices about your life. You won't find yourself stuck in an unpleasant situation because you don't have the means to support yourself. That's what Annette Fabozzi's father taught her. Fabozzi is the CEO of ICP, an information technology company, and she learned early on to make sure she could always provide for herself. "My Dad told me that I could do anything a man could do and never count on anyone but myself," she says. "He said I should get a college education and become successful for myself. Anything can happen. Even if you have a successful marriage, things can happen where you may need to take care of the family. He instilled values that I should not depend on people and be able to stand on my own."

DSC Logistics CEO Ann Drake is a member of the Committee of 200 (C200), an international not-for-profit membership association whose members consist of preeminent businesswomen who collectively control over $100 billion annually in revenue. According to Drake: "We've done studies in conjunction with the Girl Scouts and we've learned one of the reasons many women aren't going into business is because young women want to help the world and they don't see business as a way to help the world. We're trying to say if you have money then you can influence the world and have the money to spend on the world."

During a speech to the National Association of Women Business Owners in San Francisco (2006), financial guru Suze Orman said:

> I want to stop getting calls on *The Suze Orman Show* from women who are 50, 60, 70, 80 years of age telling me that their husbands walked out with the money, telling me they are now penniless and powerless because they didn't look after the money that they've brought in and worked for.

What is it going to take to instill in women the importance of being able to provide for themselves? It boils down to an issue I wrote about in my first book, and that's the undeniable fact that women are not comfortable talking about money. Ask 100 women how important making money was to them when they started their business, and I'd bet at least 80 would tell you money wasn't a motivating factor. My response typically is, if you don't want to make money with your business then volunteer with a charity or start a nonprofit organization.

Money doesn't have to be the sole reason you go into business, but it should be pretty close to the top of your list. My friend Nell Merlino and I were discussing this issue and we joked about starting a movement where we'd get women to stand up and publicly announce, "I want to make money." Pretty radical stuff, wouldn't you say?

"It's a lot easier for us to stand up and say we want to have sex than it is to say we want to make money. And consider how long that taboo was around that you couldn't talk about sex. But that is more acceptable in our society today than it is for women to talk about money," Merlino said.

Million-dollar women business owners such as Margery Kraus, CEO of APCO, don't have any qualms about making money. Kraus feels making money is the ultimate vindication:

> I don't understand why women wouldn't be as interested in this as much as men. Money is important for a couple of reasons. It provides you the security and the ability to reinvest in things you want to do, or to support philanthropic efforts, or make sure your family has what it needs. I think it is important from that point of view, but in terms of the business world it is also viewed as a measure of success. And if you're in business to be in business, it's supposed to be for profit.

I agree with her 100 percent. Making money doesn't mean you are greedy or a bad person. It represents the ability to do incredible things. Creating a company gives you a chance to play a larger part in the world. Your company becomes a separate entity from you and can reach beyond personal limitations to touch hundreds, if not millions, of people. You can better the world by creating jobs, giving back to your community, and providing products and services with the highest quality and integrity.

"If women would just internally think about the number of people they are able to employ, providing sustainable wages to those individuals, isn't that giving back? Because if you change those people's lives, you change their children's lives too," notes Cheryl Womack, chair of Leading Women Entrepreneurs of the World.™

While we are on the subject of money, one of the biggest objections I hear from women about building million-dollar businesses is that they personally don't care about becoming millionaires. That's okay. Not everyone wants to be filthy rich, but just keep in mind that owning a business that is generating $1 million in revenue doesn't mean you are personally a millionaire. In fact, in most cases, $1 million in revenue doesn't equate to $1 million in your pocket, but it does mean you *will* be comfortable. You'll also be providing employment to others. You'll be able to give back to your community. You'll be able to have an impact on the world.

Sheri Orlowitz, president of Shan Industries, a holding company that owns and operates manufacturing companies, has always been a big thinker. She doesn't shy away from the topic of money. One of her favorite people is former Bank of America chairman, Hugh McCall, who said it takes money to make a difference. As Orlowitz says:

> Money makes the world go around. It's not the only thing, but it is an essential thing. It's the oxygen of change in some respects. The personal time you devote to charitable endeavors is rewarding, but charities can't do what they do unless they have the necessary resources to be able to make a difference. I will consider myself a success when I attain a level of

financial success to be in a position to influence the social fabric of this country.

Adds Linda Drake, CEO of TCIM Services: "I think the more money you make the more money you give away. I wouldn't be in a position today to give back money to my community if I weren't making it in the first place."

Bigger Can Be Better

Does the thought of running a big company scare the daylights out of you? Perhaps you haven't pursued growth because you think the bigger your firm gets the harder you'll have to work. When you are already stressed out and working 24/7, I can understand why you'd be concerned. But let me assure you—bigger can be better.

A lot of women start businesses because they want to be in control of their own schedules and time. They want the flexibility to work hours conducive to their lifestyles. In reality though, as your business grows, you work harder and longer than you ever worked before. You reach a critical point where you'd like to hire additional help, but you aren't confident the business can sustain it. So what happens? One of three things occurs. You make the decision to back off a little. You continue to work yourself to death. Or you decide to bite the bullet—hire the additional resources and accelerate your growth.

Choosing the latter means you now have the opportunity to grow your business without killing yourself. Bigger doesn't mean more and more work heaped on top of what you already have on your plate. It means you'll gain the wherewithal to hire and purchase quality talent and resources. More assistance gives you more time to focus on your vision. There may be a slight bell curve as the company grows, but the more revenue you generate the more resources you'll have available to help you run the business.

When was the last time you had a vacation? If you did take time off, how many times did you check e-mails or call into the office? I remember the first year I was able to take a vacation without checking e-mails two or three times a day. It was liberating. I knew I had a fabulous team that was capable of managing without me. I also trusted their judgment and felt comfortable they would be in touch if there was an emergency.

When you grow your business to the next level, you'll find you don't have to burn the midnight oil every night. You'll have a social life again. You don't have to be the chief cook and bottle washer. You can step back from the day-to-day management activities. I'll talk more about the importance of letting go in Chapter 7. But suffice it to say you'll come closer to achieving the flexibility you may have been looking for when you started your business in the first place, because you have grown out of the survival mode.

Take Action: Make It Happen

I wanted to do everything everybody told me I couldn't ever do.

—Madonna

Madonna and I don't have a lot in common, but we are alike in one sense: Whenever someone tells me I can't do something, that's when I decide to show them I can. Just watch me. I set my sights on figuring out a way to make it happen. And when I figure it out, I'm determined to do it better than anyone else. You'll find the same kind of chutzpah in other successful women business owners. They know how to go out and make things happen.

Sally Hughes, CEO of Caster Connection, Inc., graduated from college and drove from Ohio to Los Angeles all alone to go after her dream of being a professional singer. "I thought, I am going to give it a try," she says.

She found jobs singing and playing her guitar in LA and Hollywood and was earning a living. She even met some famous people who took her under their wing. One mentor was swimming star, Esther Williams. "She became kind of like my surrogate mother. She really helped me along quite a bit, but I wasn't good enough and I really got burned out." So Sally loaded up her car and headed back to her parent's basement in Cleveland to figure out what she wanted to do with the rest of her life.

"I remember talking to my father and saying, 'I don't know what to do.' I had gone back to college for about three weeks thinking I'd be a school teacher, but I figured out that wasn't going to work. I couldn't imagine standing there in front of kids all day long."

Hughes' father owned a school equipment supply company, which sold everything from seat backs to locker parts. He also had a big market for chair casters. He offered Sally the opportunity to help him expand that part of his business, to which she replied, "Hello, I didn't come back from Hollywood for this."

But Hughes says one of the things she learned in LA was that she would rarely be intimidated by anyone. She knew it was a gamble but decided to give it a try. "I filled the trunk of my car. I actually was driving a station wagon back then and thought, 'Let's see what I can do with these things.'"

She drove to downtown Cleveland with her chair casters and called on maintenance men at some of the office buildings. "I asked them if the secretaries complained about their chairs not moving well and frequently they said yes. I said, 'Well I can replace the casters, and I charge $25.00.' I did the work, too. And you can imagine what these guys were thinking. I had been in LA for ten years. You can't imagine some of the outfits I showed up in."

Over the course of time, if she was going to be in this business, she was going to be the very best. That's when she decided to go after a big elephant account—General Motors. "I talked to one of the head buyers in Cleveland, and I explained I am in the caster business. I asked him how they do business. He explained to me that each plant does it individually. I said, if I consolidate it to save you significant money, would that be important to you?" That was all she needed to say to get the shot. Six months later she submitted her bid for the entire Northeast Ohio area . . . she was awarded the contract.

"I have always been a big thinker. I just didn't know how to use my talents. I just remember thinking, 'Nobody is going tell me I can't do this. I am going to do it, and I am going to be really good at it.' My father instilled this in me. Dad had polio. People always told him growing up, 'You can't do this or that,' but he'd say, 'Watch me try.' Sometimes instead of encouragement he'd say to me, 'You can't do that,' and I'd say, 'Just watch me try.'"

If at First You Don't Succeed...

Course correction is the hallmark of a mature business person. The most successful people are the ones who make lots of mistakes. They just don't make the same mistake more than once or twice.

—Author David Allen

Successful women business owners are patient, persistent, and they persevere. They know that building a great enterprise doesn't happen overnight. There's really no such thing as an overnight success. It takes time, and undoubtedly there will be a lot of No's along the way. "No" is never the end of the story in the business world. "No" is merely an obstacle in the road to maneuver around. As entrepreneurial legend Lillian Vernon, CEO and founder of Lillian Vernon Corporation, a leading national catalog and online retailer, said, "You must have a vision and passion. You must persevere. You must be optimistic, and you must never give up."[1]

Connie Rankin, president and CEO of Customized Real Estate Services in Houston, says she never takes "no" for an answer. "No can mean no for now, but it can turn into a yes down the road. One of my major corporate accounts is a Fortune 500 company. I pursued them for over four years. And they told me no for four years, but finally it was a yes," she says.

"My mother always told me, 'Where there's a will there's a way.' I've just grown up not taking no for an answer. I'm not being obnoxious about it, but I have always been pretty good at figuring out what things it takes to get to the next level, says APCO's CEO Margery Kraus.

Building a business always takes longer than you think, even with the most careful planning. There are often unanticipated expenses or changes in the market that can affect your growth strategy. There can be unforeseen circumstances that may throw you off track. You may get knocked down a time or two, but with the right attitude you can bounce back.

Even in the face of adversity, women business owners are amazingly resilient. From her vantage point, Marsha Firestone sees members of the Women Presidents' Organization who have the ability to bounce back no matter what difficult issues they confront. "When they are faced with adversity they don't back down. They don't give up and get depressed. They keep moving ahead. They are so focused and driven. Whatever obstacle they are faced with, there is nothing that stops them. They recharge, reenergize, and they keep on going like the Energizer Bunny," she says.

Trish Karter and her husband started Dancing Deer Baking Company by investing in a talented baker, Suzanne Lombardi, who had come to them for business advice. She became involved in the business and they spent five years building it together. Then the unthinkable occurred. A divorce ended not only the marital relationship and friendship, but also the business partnership. The breakup was traumatic for everyone and nearly resulted in a fold-up of the operation and personal bankruptcy

Faced with this situation, many would have thrown in the towel and given up, but Karter persevered and managed to hold the business and her life together. "To get through those tough times, I found myself putting everything through a couple of filters. One was, 'What's the best thing to do for the company and the shareholders and the employees who make this miracle happen every day?' And, the other was, 'What is the right thing for my children?' When I thought of it that way, I got up in the morning and I put my feet on the ground and I went to work, everything else came together," she says.

Creator of the pet travel bag business, Gayle Martz, got her inspiration for Sherpa bags during a difficult and tragic period in her life. "My fiancé and I were living together and we were going to get married in January. In December he died in his sleep. His will wasn't signed, and his children took everything away. I had nothing—no home, no car, no job, and no money. But I had my little dog, Sherpa, and I had my confidence. One day Sherpa and I were walking down the street and I was thinking 'Oh God, what am I going to do?' I decided to make a travel bag for Sherpa."

Martz had been a flight attendant and she knew firsthand how difficult the airlines made it for pet lovers to travel with their four-legged, furry friends. A pet travel bag was certainly a great idea, but with no money Martz didn't know how she could fund a business startup. So she went back to her previous career as a flight attendant with a paltry salary of $22,500 a year.

> I borrowed $5,000 from my mother to get started, and she became my best employee because she was willing to work for free. Together we built a business that is a global brand today. In the business world and in life we all have challenges that require that you pick yourself up and start all over again. I would say to people, when you have a delay in life, the only thing you can do is change your attitude.

Today Martz feels as though her business is her legacy to all pet lovers, because she has been successful in changing the policies concerning pet travel with all the major airlines. "My big thing was always, to do something that could make a difference in other people's lives."

The day after my partners and I purchased SBTV.com—May 2, 2003—my father suffered a massive heart attack. He was flown by a medical helicopter from his hometown in southern Missouri to Barnes-Jewish Research Hospital in St. Louis. By the time I could get there from New York, he had already been in surgery and was in intensive care. His doctors didn't give us much hope. (Happily, he's still alive today.)

So here I was with a new company and a critically ill father. A few months later my partner Dan's mother was killed instantly in a traffic accident while on vacation. It seemed as though fate was against us. But you know what? We continued to push forward. The personal trauma only made us more determined to succeed.

Believe me, I could go on and on with stories like these. So if you think life has dealt you a bad hand, think again. Remember Martz's advice. When things don't work out the way you'd like or you had planned, you can't change the situation, the only thing you can change is your attitude. You can choose to dwell on the negative and drown in your unhappiness, but that simply won't make your life any better. Go ahead and throw yourself a pity party, then get over it. Bad things happen to everyone—you're no exception. Successful happy people know how to let it go. Don't let life's disappointments and hurts prevent you from going after your dreams and living your life to the fullest. Never, never, never give up. Every day take action to make it happen.

3

GET READY,
GET SET, GROW

AS THEY SAY, timing is everything. Whether you are in the early stages of starting a business or you've decided to accelerate your business growth, building and growing the company is going to require self-sacrifice and lots of your time and your personal energy. It takes a strong constitution and stamina.

Get Your House in Order

Before you make the commitment to start or grow your business, you should get your house in order. I'm not talking about spring cleaning. If there are major issues going on in your life that require your personal attention, then it's probably not the right time to make dramatic changes in your business. Not that there aren't amazing stories of women who have built multimillion-dollar enterprises while embroiled in a personal crisis, but if you have a choice, you might as well be smart about your timing.

Start by getting your family and friends on board. Make sure they understand what it's going to be like for you, and garner their support. A strong cheering section of people who believe in you definitely gives you a leg up. Without that kind of support, the task of taking your business to the next level becomes more difficult. It's harder to stay focused when your life is filled with drama, trauma, and antagonists.

I've presented several webinars on the topic of this book. After my presentations, someone usually e-mails me with this question, "How do I deal with a spouse who doesn't support my ideas and/or business?" Unfortunately, I don't have an answer for that question. That's one you have to figure out on your own, but the question underscores the importance of getting your house in order.

Personally, I've been unbelievably lucky. My husband is an amazing supporter, mentor, and friend. There are periods when I may not see him for a couple of weeks because I'm traveling on business. Of course, when I get home I'm buried in work, not to mention being exhausted. I know he misses me not being around. All his friends have wives who have more traditional careers. But whenever I start to complain about the intense demands of the business on my time, and dream about how much I'd enjoy just a normal relaxed weekend at home, he looks at me, smiles, snickers, and says, "Yeah, right. You'd be bored to death. You are doing what you love. You wanted to build something that would be your legacy. You don't want to look back on your life with regret."

Even my father is on board. Although I am an only child and he is alone now, he never minds when the business keeps me from visiting as often as I know he and I both would like. In fact, he is so very proud of what I am doing that his friends say he brags about me all the time. I call him almost every day, and many times he ends the call by saying, "Oh, your mother would be so proud."

Women who make it to the top of the business game rarely go it alone. For example, CEO of a $70 million business, Margery Kraus, acknowledges her family has been a huge support for her. She says her family did a lot of things together in terms of domestic responsibilities, which enabled her to build her company.

"My husband and my children, from the time they were very little, chipped in at home and everybody had responsibilities. My husband is a lawyer, so he had a more predictable work schedule and was able to share some of that burden women usually have on their shoulders. But everyone in my family is very proud of what has been accomplished. It's important to me, because you can try to do a lot of things professionally at the sacrifice of your personal life, but at the end of the day it ultimately is all about family," Kraus explains.

Open communication with your family is critical. Initiate discussions and make sure everyone understands what is required of them and of you. Don't assume they will automatically know what it's going to take for you to build your business.

"You are going to come home and your mind is going to be fragmented. You're not going to be able to focus 100 percent. So just be certain that you review that with your partner," explains Peggy Mitchusson, CEO of The Face and The Body Day Spas.

The first year Mitchusson started her business, she thought she had it all together. She had done all the right preparation work to make the business successful, except for one important thing. She hadn't really discussed the ramifications of the demands the business would place on her marriage. Returning home one evening after a 12-hour day, her husband announced he wanted a divorce.

"He said, 'You are never here, and you are distracted when I am talking to you.' He explained he felt as though I wasn't available for him, and quite honestly I made a decision to fix those things. We didn't get a divorce. Thankfully, we worked through it, but I am just saying I didn't realize how I was neglecting him. But I did also have his support, meaning he was willing to come half way because he was an entrepreneur, too. We knew that this was going to change our lives, and it did. We both adjusted to it because we were both willing to make some compromises. But there had to be something left when I got home. I would not have been able to see the business through difficult challenges if I had been too stressed or had not had the support at home," Mitchusson adds.

Having been a stay-at-home mom for nine years, Bonny Filandrinos decided when her two sons were ages 10 and 15 it was time to do something for herself. She decided to launch her company, Staffing Solutions. As she explains:

> I sat my family down and explained to them that things were going to change. I explained that it was going to be time consuming for a while, and I asked for assistance and support. I wanted my husband and sons to become a little more self-sufficient, less dependent on me, and more willing to share the management of the household. I didn't get that support. My now ex-husband expected me to continue as if nothing was different, and I resented that. I had invested nine years of my life being a stay-at-home mom supporting my husband in his career growth, and I felt it was my turn.

Linda Drake, CEO of TCIM Services, an international information services company focusing on customer care and customer acquisition for Fortune 100 companies, recommends involving your spouse, significant other, or life partner in the development of your business plan. "This allows your spouse to be invested in the dream and it allows you both to make decisions ahead of time regarding childcare, household chores, and meals."

Relationships May Change: Be Prepared

Surround yourself only with people who are going to lift you higher.
—Oprah Winfrey

This is a difficult subject to address, but nonetheless one I find to be necessary. Because a lot of women spend far too much time worrying about what other people think, it's natural for them to be concerned about how their business success could affect their personal relationships. In fact, this is such a tough topic that when I interviewed women and asked them about this subject, they were always a bit reluctant to talk about it.

In an ideal world, you would be as successful as your heart desired and everyone you know would stand up and applaud you—be happy for you. But we don't live in an ideal world, and the bottom line is, not everyone is going to be thrilled for you. So you can't be naïve and assume your relationships will remain status quo. You need to acknowledge going in that some of your relationships may change. Some may not. But keep in mind you'll also discover new, wonderful relationships along the way.

So let's start with our spouses, life partners, or significant others. One of my favorite coffee mugs says, "Behind every great woman is a man who is surprised." Yes, it's worth a chuckle, but as they say, there is truth in jest.

Did you know that 32 percent of working women earn more than their husbands?[1] It is an interesting dynamic and one that can negatively affect a relationship. It really depends on the two individuals.

Women who start businesses and grow them to amazing heights are often surprised to find their spouses unenthusiastic. That may be disheartening at first, but let me assure you that most women who find themselves in a situation where their husbands can't deal with their success recognize it never was a relationship made in heaven. If that person you have chosen to share your life with can't take pride in your success and share in your happiness, then you really need to examine whether that's the right relationship for you.

"When you marry you either grow together, or you grow apart. If you don't see the potential in the other person to change, and if that wasn't part of your paradigm when you married, you get into trouble. If you have this preconceived notion that you are going to stay in a steady state forever, it's a problem, because nothing is a steady state," explains Linda Drake.

Sally Hughes, the caster queen, married a successful man who couldn't accept her own business success. Sadly, the marriage ended in a painful divorce, but she says, looking back, "It was the best thing that ever happened to me. The Lord was looking down on me that day. I have been remarried for about ten years now, and I have a supportive husband. Plus, I have a seven-year-old child."

For Avis Yates Rivers, CEO of Technology Concepts, her first marriage ended as she was growing her wildly successful company. "I hired my first husband for the business. He came in one day and looked around and saw I had a multimillion-dollar operation with lots of employees, and he thought he could add something to it. Not every man is built to be married to a woman who is very determined and very aggressive and not willing to let anything get in the way."

Kathleen Thurmond took over her father's business, Best Washington, after he had a stroke. Six months after she took the reins, her husband died, leaving her alone to raise her 6-year-old daughter. Kathleen then met someone else who stepped into her life and did a wonderful job of blending into the family—for a while anyway. As the business grew, Kathleen began to do some innovative things that positioned her as a leader in her industry. She had lots of publicity, and there was an enthusiastic buzz in the market about her company.

"The more success we had, the more I realized I needed to go back to school and complete my MBA. When I finished in 2003, he decided to leave. He couldn't handle it anymore. It definitely wasn't easy, but I have great friends, particularly great women friends, and it really sustained me through all of this," Thurmond says.

It's not only the relationship you share with your spouse or partner that may change. Friendships may change as well. Long-time friends may have difficulty accepting you in your new role. You may not have as much in common as you used to. Because of the demands of your business, you probably won't have as much time to socialize, and some in your social circle may become offended and cut you off.

There are some relationship changes you can manage. For example, it's okay if some friends don't understand the challenges you face with your business. So don't be hurt or frustrated when they aren't interested in talking about the issues you confront or the stresses you have at work. Just enjoy their company and friendship for what it is.

After twenty successful years in business, Julie Levi, president of Progressive Promotions, says her marriage and her friends have happily stayed intact. "But I don't think my friends have any idea of the affluence I've acquired because of my business, and that's fine. It's important to remain humble and grateful for everything you have," she says.

Mary Quigg has seen her friendships change over the years, although she has kept several friends who will always be good friends. "We just don't talk about business," she says.

But sadly, there are friends, particularly women friends, who will resent and be jealous of your success. And it may surprise you the lengths to which some are willing to go to take away from your success. When I wrote my first book, I enjoyed reading the reviews as they appeared on Amazon.com. Writing a book is a little like exposing your soul, so I was pleased to see favorable comments. Then one evening my husband and I came home from dinner and I decided to check one more time. When I scrolled down, I was horrified to find a new review written by Anonymous from Anywhere, U.S.A. The comments were vitriolic. Much of the information contained in the review was information only someone who knew me well would know, because it wasn't anywhere to be found in the book. I was hurt and extremely upset.

"Why would someone say such horrible things about me?" I asked my husband. With a frown on his face, he replied, "Susan, practice what you preach."

He was referring to the countless times I have coached women not to allow other people to have power over you. My reaction to the review was exactly what this individual—and I imagine it was a woman—wanted it to be. Hurt. Disbelief. Self-doubt.

So I quickly got back in control of my feelings and wrote Amazon.com to explain the unfairness of the review, because the comments were based on information that went beyond the scope of the book. Amazon agreed and removed it from the site, apologizing for letting it slip through. I also realized the review really wasn't about me. It was a projection of the insecurity of someone who obviously wasn't very happy with herself.

That's not the first time something like this has happened, and it won't be the last. A reporter who was writing an article about me asked me whether there were people who would like to see me fail.

"You bet there are," I replied. You see, as long as you are succeeding and living your life in an extraordinary way, there will be those who will resent you. They are typically people who aren't willing to exert the effort to excel themselves—but they are ready to spend the energy trying to knock you down. Ignore them. Don't give them any power over your life.

Keep this in mind. You are the same person you have always been. If people can't accept you and take joy in your success, then it's their problem not yours. Don't let them rain on your parade. This is your time to shine, and you deserve it.

Those who truly love you will always love you and you will love them back.

Create a Peer Support Network

Whether it's dealing with business growth or personal relationships, creating a strong peer network you can count on can have a tremendous impact on your ability to travel down the million-dollar path successfully. When you are leading an organization, you often feel isolated and alone. Sometimes you feel as though the weight of the world is on your shoulders and you are the only one who has ever experienced the problems you are having. When you cultivate a group of friends who are in similar positions, you'll have an inherent support group to help guide you.

I have been fortunate to gain the friendship of some of the most amazing women in this country, if not the world. I am fortunate not only to know them, but to have benefited from their guidance and support. It's the best group of advisors anyone could ask for.

You can build your own informal peer support network, but you can also take advantage of formal peer advisory groups, which can nurture your business growth and allow you to build strong bonds of friendship, such as Vistage International and the Young Entrepreneurs' Organization. Additionally, many local business organizations have created peer advisory roundtables. These groups can serve as a sounding board, help you handle personal issues, overcome isolation, and improve your overall odds of success.

Kay Koplovitz, founder and former chairman and CEO of USA Networks, says, "Although I have joined other types of organizations, such as media trade groups usually open to all in an industry, it is in the peer-to-peer groups, whose membership is selective and often by invitation only, where I have found the support necessary to function effectively as an entrepreneur."[2]

As I mentioned in the Introduction, I belong to the Women Presidents' Organization, which is a peer advisory group exclusively for women with multimillion-dollar businesses. I enjoy the "women only" aspect of this organization because the dynamics of a group change when only women are in the room. You can share details you wouldn't be comfortable discussing in a mixed group. For example, my group completely understands when someone sheds a few tears and needs to talk about PMS, mood swings, or hot flashes. We're just as likely to focus on a member's family problems as we are their business concerns, because for us our personal and business lives are intertwined. If men were at these meetings, how often do you think that would happen?

As Caryn Burstein, who is president of the interior architectural and design firm, CLB Interiors, explains, "WPO is an incredible organization. It allows me and other women in the community who are in noncompetitive firms to really open up and discuss business issues. I never really had a mentor or anybody to look up to, and this is a group of enthusiastic, powerful women. It's a great learning experience. The greatest thing is you can open up and talk about issues in your business and have someone else console you and say, 'I've been there. I've done that, and this is what you need to do to save time, effort, and energy."

According to Jennifer DeNyse, CEO of DeNyse Signs, a twenty-one-year-old company with over ninety employees that makes signs for large companies:

> There are so many things that you gain. One is the sharing of information so valuable that only owners can know it. There are certain innate differences between being an owner and just a management level individual—the information you process each day and the types of employee issues and the types of financial issues that you don't get any other way than by being an owner. And the sharing of that information and the resources you can gain from swapping information is just incredible.

As the CEO of one of the few women-led firms to receive venture capital investment, Gail Goodman of Constant Contact finds her peer advisory group to be a great investment of her time. They meet for a day and a half each quarter, and the other members are all CEOs of venture-backed companies. "I am the only woman, but I strongly recommend it," she says.

Most peer advisory groups require you to meet certain criteria in order to be accepted as a member, and the membership fees can range from $700 to as much as $10,000 per year. But it is well worth the investment of your time and money.

Mentors Can Guide Your Growth

Mentoring is a term historically used to describe a teacher-student relationship. In the business world, mentoring occurs when a more experienced professional (the mentor) gives significant career assistance to a less-experienced professional (the protégé). Mentoring relationships are particularly helpful during a period of transition, such as a new business launch, a new product introduction, or a business expansion. A mentor's knowledge, experience, tenacity, and skills offer the growing entrepreneur guidance, advice, and training.

Some of today's most established women business owners say they never had a mentor as they were building their businesses, but they recognize what a tremendous help it would have been to have one.

The Center for Women's Business Research conducted a study of women-owned firms who were mentored through the Women's Business Centers from January 2001 to October 2003. The study demonstrated the important role mentors play in business success. Women's Business Centers, a program of the U.S. Small Business Administration, represent a national network of more than eighty educational centers designed to assist women who want to start and grow small businesses. Women's Business Centers operate with the mission to level the playing field for women entrepreneurs who still face unique obstacles in the world of business.

"Over the course of the study, women business owners were increasingly likely to characterize their businesses as experiencing rapid growth rather than as stable or declining," said Myra M. Hart, chair of the Center for Women's Business Research and professor at the Harvard Business School. "Clearly, mentoring, and training can provide important tools for women engaged in launching new ventures or nurturing high growth businesses. *One can learn how to be an entrepreneur.*"[3]

Overall, the women entrepreneurs in the study reported a substantial increase in their key business skills. Improvement was also observed in such skills as having a clear business vision and detailed financial plan, being able to describe one's average customer, knowing how to seek business capital, and using business skills in other areas of one's life.

Denise Houseberg founded MarketExpo.com, a successful mini-version of Amazon.com that showcases entire product lines of thirty-four manufacturers—items ranging from hardware to furnishing and more. In 2005, she was given a mentor when she was chosen as an award recipient in the "Make Mine a $Million Business" program. "My mentor challenged me to take a broader view of my business. Having a mentor who as an outsider had gone through the same growth challenges I was experiencing went a long way in helping me see the big picture." Denise says it helped her expand her vision and widen her scope which helped her believe in her future success. As a result, she became the first awardee to hit her goal of $1 million in sales—passing this milestone just six months after receiving the award.

Julie Levi, president of Progressive Promotions, is one of the "Make Mine a $Million Business" mentors. Even though she never had a mentor in business, she finds it rewarding to help other women business owners grow. "We meet at least once a month and talk about all aspects of her business. We look at her marketing, her finances, and we look for strategies to accelerate her growth," she says.

Since January, Clarice Kennedy has been mentoring Maureen Borzacchiello, CEO of Creative Display Solutions. Clarice's company posted 2005 revenues of $12 million. Maureen has a strong background in the trade show and exhibit display industry, and Clarice was immediately impressed with her level of enthusiasm, energy, and knowledge of her industry.

"We immediately set both business and personal goals for the upcoming year and worked on prioritizing them. Hiring a sales team and working on a compensation plan was at the top of Maureen's list. I was able to share my experience at setting sales goals based on gross profit (bottom line) and not on the top line. Maureen was able to take the model and incorporate it into her compensation plan for her sales team," Clarice notes.

She adds, "As business owners, regardless of the size of our businesses, we all have the same issues. I certainly don't have all the answers, but I can share what has worked for my business and what has not and hopefully give Maureen another perspective—business owner to business owner.[4]

There are formal programs such as the "Make Mine a $Million Business" program or the Women's Business Centers, where you can find mentors. But there are also more informal mentor relationships that occur naturally. As you meet other business owners you respect and admire, don't be embarrassed to ask for their input. Most people are flattered when you ask their opinion. Your mentor doesn't have to look like you either. However, if someone becomes your mentor be prepared to listen and learn. Don't be defensive. Keep an open mind.

PART TWO

Using the Four Strategic Keys
to Growing Your Business

STRATEGICALLY THERE are four key areas for growing your business:

1. Creating the mission and vision of your company

2. Developing a scalable business model with the right team

3. Creating unique market strategies

4. Obtaining the necessary funding

Transitioning your business from a startup to a growing enterprise requires the development of more sophisticated operating procedures. As the owner of a startup, you are a hands-on operator.

You make the sales calls, fulfill the contracts, send out the invoices, make collection calls, answer the phone, and empty the waste baskets. You are the business. Entrepreneurs thrive on juggling a lot of balls in the air—it's exciting. They enjoy having total control over every aspect of the business so they can do it exactly the way they want to do it.

A growing organization can't "manage by the seat of its pants." As you build your million-dollar business, your organization needs to develop an infrastructure with formal policies, procedures and processes. I'm not suggesting you create an inflexible corporate bureaucracy, but you need to make sure you have some structure in place so your business won't become a house of cards.

4

CREATE THE VISION

BURIED IN THE day-to-day operations of the company, it's easy to get tunnel vision about your business. Your nose is to the grindstone everyday—getting it done. Such a limited perspective may be the biggest reason business owners fail to seize growth opportunities. Myopic vision limits your ability to think about the big picture.

Before your business can grow, you should be able to articulate a clear vision of where it is you want your company to go. Sounds simplistic, doesn't it? It's not.

Define the Vision of Your Company

A business without a dream is like a life without a purpose.

—Michael Gerber

A *vision statement* is sometimes referred to as a picture of your company in the future but it's really so much more than that. Your vision statement is your dream—your inspiration, the framework for all your strategic planning.

To create the vision for your business step away from and take a fresh look at your company. What's happening in the world today? What are the market trends? This is your chance to gaze into your crystal ball and see into the future. Imagine there aren't any constraints such as money, people or resources. What direction would you take? What will your business look like? The vision is all about what it is you are going to do—not how you are going to do it. It's not about execution.

I find it helpful to get away from the business for a few days in order to think about the vision of my company. You also might go on a retreat with some of your key advisors or employees and spend the time brainstorming. If that's impossible, at least get away from your work environment. I'm sure you know there are far too many distractions there to think about vision.

Michael Gerber, who is a well-known small business expert, has a new program he calls "In the Dreaming Room: Awakening the Entrepreneur in You" (www.inthedreamingroom.com). The program consists of a weekend seminar designed to be a place where entrepreneurs can practice a new kind of dreaming he calls "intentional dreaming"®—which has nothing to do with problem solving and everything to do with transforming your whole life and business in a radically creative and strategic way. According to Gerber:

> The surprising reason that most small businesses fail is not because their dream is too big, but rather too small, too realistic—it isn't big enough to sustain more life.

Talk to people outside your company and ask them what they see. When you are entrenched in the daily operations, you might be missing revenue and market opportunities because you simply don't see them. You may be amazed at some of the growth- and revenue-generating ideas that are right under your nose.

As a certified business coach, Dresdene Flynn-White, has seen this several times. "Often the owner is so entrenched in the activities necessary to keep the business alive, they have little time to focus on generating ideas to move the business forward. One situation that comes to mind is a restaurant whose name and theme suggested a fairly specialized and restricted menu. The reality was, the restaurant had a full menu and catering services with a certain type of food as their specialty," she says.

Flynn-White says the restaurant was suffering from limited traffic based on the perception they only sold one type of food. "One thing that was obvious to me, and which was immediately implemented, was vivid and attractive pictures of the variety of menu offerings. These were displayed on the tables and the walls so that patrons were made aware of the additional menu and services. Not rocket science, something simple but important for the business to move forward," she adds.

Don't rob yourself of the time you need to create your vision. Once you have defined your vision, your next challenge as a leader is to articulate your vision to your team and get them to embrace it, as well. Everyone within your organization needs to understand where the company is heading and how he or she can help.

Articulate Your Mission

Once you've envisioned the future and you know in which direction you want your business to go, it's time to create a mission statement and a value statement. These become the foundation for everything else you do in your company. Together, they define the strategic strengths of your company. They also establish the character and voice of your brand, and articulate where you are headed.

A mission statement is a brief description of a company's fundamental purpose. A mission statement answers the question, "Why do we exist?" The difference between a mission and vision statement is that the mission statement focuses on the present state of your business, whereas the vision statement focuses on the future.

A *mission statement* should never be more than a few sentences that define what your company delivers to your customers, employees and the community. To draft a mission statement, start by listing your organization's strengths and keys to success. Then, think about how your business relates to the marketplace. List all these qualities, and then select your top three or four and begin to formulate sentences that describe the core essence of your firm. Don't throw something together that really says nothing about who you are and what you do. A mission statement isn't rhetoric. It isn't something you write down and never refer to again. It's an important element of your business, and it should be treated as such. Here are two good examples of mission statements from some well-known companies:

> *Otis Elevator:* To provide any customer a means of moving people and things up, down and sideways over short distances with higher reliability than any similar enterprise in the world.

> *Courtyard by Marriott:* To provide economy and quality minded travelers with a premiere, moderate priced lodging facility which is consistently perceived as clean, comfortable, well-maintained and attractive, staffed by friendly, attentive and efficient people.

These examples clearly articulate what business the company is in, what their promise to their customers is, and what is expected of their employees.

Communicate the Core Values

Your growing company also needs a *value statement*. A value statement not only says what your company stands for, but it also creates the character and voice of your company. It helps employees and customers understand the type of company with which they are dealing. These values should be never be compromised under any circumstances.

Melanie Bergeron, who now runs Two Men and a Truck, says she worked with her team and came up with the following core values to help define their company in a competitive market:

Integrity: To always conduct oneself with honesty and fairness.

Give Back to the Community: A portion of every move the system completes is donated to the American Cancer Society.

The Grandma Rule®: To treat everyone the way you would want your Grandma to be treated.

Be Your Best and Have Fun: To be the best professionally and personally while enjoying life and having fun.

Inclusion: To welcome people from all backgrounds in the workplace and the community.

These five values are such an integral part of the company's culture that Melanie has incorporated them into their marketing campaign by creating this slogan:

Two Men and a Truck® is not just a moving company—it's a customer service company that moves.

Of course, once you have completed the drafting of your mission and value statements, they need to become a permanent part of your company's culture. It's vitally important to get all your employees to embrace them and make them a part their day-to-day activities. They are the heart and soul of your business.

Donna Vandiver, CEO of the Vandiver Group, a strategic marketing and public relations firm, understands the importance of getting buy-in from her employees. "We have a retreat each January to go over our mission, vision, and values statements. We hold quizzes during the year for football tickets or a free lunch or dinner for the most correct answers about our clients, our own mission/vision, values, etc. I think this keeps it fresh and tells people we want to live it. We include it in our strategic plan each year, which all employees get a copy of, and it is on our website."

At Dancing Deer, Trish Karter's idealistic vision is part of her company's culture: "As an organization, we are trying to do something a lot bigger than making great cakes and cookies. We often times think of it as selling good karma by encouraging our values of environmentalism, purity in food, respect and a positive working environment."

In 1997, Dancing Deer Baking Company was offered an amazing opportunity, but the company turned it down because of its commitment to its core values. Williams-Sonoma asked if Dancing Deer could supply molasses-clove cookies to their 165 kitchen wares stores. Despite the promise of massive exposure, Trish said "no" because Williams-Sonoma required a product with a four-month shelf-life. Dancing Deer uses perishable, all-natural ingredients, which wouldn't have worked. But the buyer called Trish back and said, "I respect your values. How about a gingerbread mix?" The deal was done, and in fact, mixes have been a growth area of the company ever since.

Great companies don't compromise when it comes to their mission, vision, and values. One great brand that has become part of our country's culture is Steinway Pianos. I purchased a Steinway grand piano recently, and I had the opportunity to tour their factory. It is truly amazing. Practically everything is done the way it has been done since the company was founded in 1858—almost entirely by hand. There aren't any short cuts or compromises, and quality is the focus of every employee. Steinway could have easily transitioned over the years to pre-fabricated pieces manufactured by machines and ramped up its production. Instead, the company manufactures only a few thousand pianos each year, and each one takes about fourteen months from start to finish. Today, the brand is synonymous with quality because the company has remained true to its mission and core values of producing the finest instrument in the world.

Create the Right Business Plan

It takes as much energy to wish as it does to plan.

—Eleanor Roosevelt

Business plans have been referred to as the water for a thirsty plant. They keep businesses alive, thriving, and vital. If they have a plan at all, many entrepreneurs keep it in their heads and never take the time to write it down. There's a television commercial where the wife points to her husband's head and says, "Our sales figures are all in there." That's pretty typical. Entrepreneurs often manage with a "fly by the seat of your pants" approach, relying on their street smarts and intuition. If that has worked for you so far—that's great. Good for you. But listen to me carefully. If you don't plan for growth, you may grow, but it's unlikely you can sustain it.

Have you ever seen a chicken slaughtered for Sunday dinner? Well, I have. I grew up in the country, and I spent quite a bit of time on a farm when I was a little girl, so I had the opportunity to watch this activity a number of times. When you cut off a chicken's head, you have to hold on really tight, because if you don't it will get away from you and start flapping around all over the barn yard. Although the headless chicken stirs up quite a ruckus, I guarantee you it is dead.

You might wonder where I'm going with this crazy story. Well, it's a simple analogy. If you don't plan for your business growth, it's just like that chicken. You might flap around for awhile, but your company will be just as dead as the beheaded bird. Planning for growth is essential. According to a PricewaterhouseCoopers survey, two-thirds of CEOs of fast-growth companies report having some type of growth plan in place.[1]

Former President Dwight D. Eisenhower once said, "Plans are nothing; planning is everything." The exercise of drafting your plan is more important than the actual plan itself, because it makes you think through the next steps and focus on your strategies, expenses, revenues, and profitability. When I look back on some of the initial business plans we wrote for SBTV.com, I have to chuckle. While our core business strategy has stayed on target, our business has evolved and matured over time. Some of the ideas we had early on just didn't work or ended up not making sense. A good business plan isn't meant to be written once and never touched again. It changes as your business changes and evolves. The value of writing the business plan is the actual exercise of writing it.

....
ELEMENTS OF A BUSINESS PLAN

Executive Summary: The executive summary is the most important section of your business plan. It provides a concise overview of the entire plan along with a history of your company.

Market Analysis: The market analysis section should illustrate your knowledge about the particular industry your business is in. It should also present general highlights and conclusions of any marketing research data you have collected; however, the specific details of your marketing research studies should be moved to the appendix section of your business plan.

Company Description: Without going into detail, this section should include a high-level look at how all of the different elements of your business fit together. The company description section should include information about the nature of your business as well as list the primary factors that you believe will make your business a success.

Organization and Management: This section should include your company's organizational structure, details about the ownership of your company, profiles of your management team, and the qualifications of your board of directors.

Marketing and Sales Strategies: Marketing is the process of creating customers, and customers are the lifeblood of your business. In this section, the first thing you must do is define your marketing strategy. There is no single way to approach a marketing strategy; your strategy should be part of an ongoing self-evaluation process and unique to your company. However, there are steps you can follow that will help you think through the strategy you would like to use.

Service or Product Line: What are you selling? In this section, describe your service or product, emphasizing the benefits to potential and current customers. For example, don't tell your readers which eighty-nine foods you carry in your "Gourmet to Go" shop. Tell them why busy, two-career couples will prefer shopping in a service-oriented store that records clients' food preferences and caters even the smallest parties on short notice.

Funding Request: In this section, request the amount of funding you will need to start or expand your business. If necessary, include different funding scenarios, such as a best- and a worst-case scenario, but remember that later, in the financial section, you must be able to back up these requests and scenarios with corresponding financial statements.

Financials: Develop the financials after you've analyzed the market and set clear objectives. That's when you can allocate resources efficiently. This usually includes three to five years of historical data.

The Internet provides excellent resources to help you write your business plan. There are also business plan software packages you can purchase or download. In general, here are some of the questions you'll need to answer in order to write a solid plan:

- ➤ Who are your customers and why do they need your product or service?

- ➤ What problem are you solving, or what void are you filling?

- ➤ What's the market opportunity? What is the size of the market?

- ➤ What is your unique value proposition?

- ➤ Who is the competition?

- ➤ How do you differentiate yourself?

- ➤ How defensible is your business?

- ➤ How profitable can this business be? Is it scalable?

- ➤ What are your growth strategies? Are they feasible?

- ➤ What are your financial projections?

- ➤ How much capital will you need, and how will you use those funds?

In addition to helping you manage the growth of your business, your business plan is also an important measurement tool. It should serve as a gauge by which you measure your progress. WPO's founder Marsha Firestone advises setting up a measurement system to gauge monthly, quarterly, and annual results. "Then, make certain the day-to-day tactics employed by your staff are connected with the long-term vision," she adds.

With her company's twenty-two offices and over $35 million in annual revenues, Liz Elting, cofounder of TransPerfect Translations, has plotted her course since day one. She believes in yearly company evaluations with her staff. "We set goals for ourselves, and at the end of the year, we see how we did. It's good to have a long-term business plan as you start, but you also need annual goals," she explains.[2]

A business plan can help you weigh opportunities so you can make better-informed decisions. The plan will also position you to be more proactive with your business strategy, rather than reactive. Just think of it as a blueprint for your company. Certainly, you may adjust and tweak things along the way, but at least you have direction.

You'll need a business plan if you require funding to execute your growth objectives. Whether you are seeking debt or equity financing, you'll be asked to present a business plan that demonstrates exactly how you are going to use the funds and what return you'll achieve on that investment.

We'll talk more about money for growth in Chapter 7. For now, suffice it to say that you can't escape the need to draft a business plan, but remember, it's a business tool with a variety of helpful uses.

Focus, Focus, Focus

Once you have your plan in place, stay focused. Most people don't lack opportunity, they lack focus. Entrepreneurs are deal doers. We see opportunities, and we want to run with them. But winding up with too many irons in the fire can be the death of any organization— regardless of how small or large.

Your focus should always be on businesses or products that complement, or are synergistic with your existing business. Moving into unrelated businesses where you have no experience or expertise can be disastrous. As Marsha Firestone says:

> I have seen so many women make mistakes by going in too many directions simultaneously and using up their resources

and failing in all categories. I think that once the mission is defined, a woman business owner, and for that matter any business owner, should really stay focused on what is the most important product or service they are selling.

"The times I have gotten into trouble are when I diverted from my plan. An example would be: We plan to diversify right now and to go into a slightly different type of spa—a medical spa. As I investigate, I see so many other things that are appealing, so many opportunities—Oh, why don't you try this, or Why don't you try that? And it's provocative. But my advice is to stick to your plan," says the CEO of The Face and The Body Spa, Peggy Mitchusson.

You can't be all things to all people. Every time you say "yes" to one thing, you are effectively saying "no" to something else. As you grow and expand your business, you need to make sure your resources are spent on those activities which will help you achieve your objectives.

Finally, you must have buy-in. No plan can be successfully executed without the buy-in of your entire company. Include key members of your team in the plan's development so everyone in the company has a vested interest in its success. Pushing a plan down from the top never works. Your team will easily find reasons why the plan won't work. Without buy-in you'll find it extremely difficult if not impossible to succeed. Make sure your staff is signed up and ready to grow!

Invest in Professional Resources and Advisors

If I were to venture a guess, I'd say more than 80 percent of business startups don't utilize professional resources and advisors. They either set themselves up as a sole proprietorship, or incorporate themselves on line without any legal advice. They handle their own accounting and they file their own taxes. They even serve as their own creative department, designing business cards, letterhead, brochures, and websites.

One of the smartest things you can do when building a company is to invest in expert resources. Trying to save money by managing your own legal, financial, even marketing needs will undoubtedly cost you more in the long run.

Consider Poppy Gall and Carolyn Cooke's $4 million-plus company, Isis, which manufactures a line of outerwear for active women. The company's original name was "Juno," but they were hit with a cease-and-desist order because there was a plus-size women's clothing company with the same name. If Poppy and Carolyn had reached out for professional assistance and paid the $1,000 it cost to check whether the name was trademarked, it would have saved them $25,000 in legal and design fees.[3]

Similarly, with no money for an attorney, Gayle Martz filed her own patents and trademarks for her pet travel bags. She remembers the day an article came out about her company in *Travel and Leisure* magazine. It was an exciting day, to be sure, to get such great publicity for her young company, until a cease-and-desist letter was delivered to her door demanding she destroy all her bags. As she advises:

> Always protect yourself with the professionals you need to help you fight off those who are trying to take it all away.

According to research from the Center for Women's Business Research, successful women-owned firms are more likely to use professional advisors and develop outside sources—such as a board of directors or an advisory board—to gain an outsider's perspective and create greater accountability.

Growing businesses need to be managed in a more formal fashion to deal with the increased numbers of customers, vendors, and employees. You also need professional advice to protect your business interests. According to attorney Meryl Lynn Unger, who is a partner with Katsky Korins LLP in New York:

> In a competitive business environment, where information can be easily transmitted electronically and where employees are increasingly mobile, I counsel my clients to protect their most valuable assets—intellectual property and other proprietary information—by creating and implementing preventive measures. These strategies include policies and contracts which are designed to safeguard the company's valuable information from unlawful use or disclosure by current or former employees and consultants: they can also deter raiding of the company's employees and customers by former employees and consultants.

"Some of the most successful programs we have developed for our clients," Unger continues, "arose after a company's misfortune of having employees leave, starting a competitive business, and raiding other employees; or of having a top salesperson leave to join a competitor and then solicit the company's customers on behalf of the competitor. In those instances, the companies were highly motivated to put in place a carefully constructed program of policies and contracts, and to communicate to their staff the compelling business reasons for such a program. Of course, an ounce of prevention is worth a pound of cure, and companies that implement these programs pre-emptively have found them to be cost-effective and powerful tools to protect their business interests."

There is no doubt professional advice early on can pay huge dividends for your growing company. Avis Yates Rivers, CEO of Technology Concepts Group, regrets not having a broader spectrum of advisors as she grew her company. "In retrospect, had I hooked up with some innovators of products and software, and then attracted equity capital, we could have been Google," she says.

Mary Quigg, CEO of Vandover Group, also regrets not having good advisors. She says: "Clear role definition and good advisors early on would have made a huge difference. Optimism doesn't compensate for lack of capital, and we were very optimistic, but we didn't have enough money to fund the business the way it needed to be funded on the front end. Good advisors, a formal business plan and a solid banking relationship from day one would have made a huge difference."

Remember, however, not all advisors are created equal. Consultants, coaches and financial advisors don't necessarily need a license or any sort of certification. "Just about anyone with some business experience and a website can hold themselves out as a 'consultant' or 'coach' these days, so before hiring any sort of business advisor, make sure you are comfortable the person will actually add value and help improve your business performance," says attorney, SBTV.com legal contributor, and syndicated columnist Cliff Ennico.

Step Up to the Role of CEO

Being a CEO is more than having the title printed on your business card. As you grow your million-dollar enterprise, you need to act, look, think, and *be* the CEO. Some women find that a difficult transition and a challenging role.

When your company is small, your staff is very much like your family. In fact, some of them may actually be family members. Everyone goes out to lunch together or they all get together for happy hour after work. You may be the CEO and owner, but you are also one of the gang.

As the CEO of a million-dollar-plus business, you are the spokesperson, the visionary and the leader. Like it or not, you should distance yourself from the troops. Don't take that the wrong way. You can be accessible, but access should be more limited. You can't be one of the gang anymore, and you must communicate that. Not an easy thing to do.

Pamela Chambers O'Rourke's firm, ICON Information Consultants, is now a $57 million business. Pamela is one of the most personable people I know. I'd describe her as a bubbly, cute, southern blonde. She's not someone who would come to mind when you think of a typical CEO, but she is an extremely successful and savvy businesswoman. She admits it's lonely at the top.

"I had to grow into the CEO position. I had to learn to remove myself from my staff. I can't be the person who always goes out with everyone. I can be cordial, and I can occasionally do things, like go out for cocktails. But I have to limit my drinks to two, and I have to watch everything I do," she says.

Peggy Mitchusson of The Face and The Body Day Spas, which does about $8 million in annual revenue, agrees. She started her company small. She did a lot of the facial work herself, and she realized several years into the business that she couldn't be the CEO of the company and be doing service all day. So she quit doing treatments and became the true CEO of her firm.

"And guess what, my staff was really better than me. We started growing, and I had to start thinking like an employer instead of one of the staff. I had to position myself to be objective. Now I make decisions based on the facts and what the numbers say rather than personalities," Mitchusson explains.

CEO of venture-backed Constant Contact, Gail Goodman remembers that as the business grew and changed, she had to change with it:

I felt like when we started I was the central glue. I knew everyone's name. I was the doer and the decision maker. Now, I have no operational responsibilities and I see myself more as a coach and a mentor. I am the keeper of the culture and chief communicator.

According to Ann Drake, CEO of DSC Logistics: "Being an entrepreneur is one thing, but taking your business to the next level, that's another. Finding and hiring the right staff to help a company grow, and managing the company through those employees are among the challenges you'll face as CEO."

Keep in mind, when you take that step into the role of CEO, there are going to be employees who don't like you. Yes, when they are gathered around the coffee machine, they are probably talking about you. Don't let it drive you crazy. Business is business and friendship is friendship. Don't ever forget that. As actress Kirstie Alley says, "You are not in business to be popular."[4]

Build an Advisory Board

Growing a business today is complex. The more information, talent, and resources you can access, the greater your chances of success. Advisory boards can help. No matter how small or large your firm is, you can benefit from building an advisory board.

Think about the last time you met with other business people and had an open discussion, sharing your ideas and concerns. An advisory board is a formal version of this process.

Susan Stautberg is president of PartnerCom, a New York company that helps businesses globally to set up advisory boards to suit their individual needs. Stautberg says creating an advisory board is a cost-effective way to gain critical expertise in areas that may be outside the company's core competency. "As opposed to corporate boards, which are more public, advisory boards give a company the opportunity to change focus as needed," she says.

Advisory boards bring talent, ideas and contacts to your business, but unlike corporate boards they don't have any fiduciary or legal liability because they provide nonbinding advice. That means they are not required to maintain Directors & Officers insurance.

Business success can bring on managerial blindness—the notion that if it worked in the past, it will continue to work in the future. "Advisors help you move beyond this limited vision and break out of the cycle of mediocrity based on unimaginative benchmarking and simple imitation of rivals," Stautberg explains.

Determine how many people you want to serve on your board. Having too many people often results in a lack of productivity. Consider having two or three people and choose wisely. Selecting the right individuals for your board is critical. In order to make the right choices, you should consider your personal skills and strengths. Make a list of the areas in your business where you need the most help. Use this list to identify advisory board members who can complement your attributes. Remember to look for people who are strong enough to take unpopular stances and give you honest feedback. It's critical your board members understand the dynamics of a small business and the challenges of your industry. You should also consider whether you are truly willing to listen to advice that runs counter to your ideas.

"Entrepreneurs are often contrarians who believe they can succeed no matter the pitfalls and who may not want to hear opposing views," notes Bob Brockhaus, Ph.D., who has worked with start-up companies for more than thirty-two years. He held the Coleman Foundation Chair in Entrepreneurship at Saint Louis University's John Cook School of Business, where he was also the director of the Jefferson Smurfit Center for Entrepreneurial Studies. He finds many entrepreneurs are so confident in their enterprise they overlook essential information.

"There are always different points of view, particularly if the people on your advisory board are experienced in something you don't have much experience in, like corporate finance. The idea is to get the input, but ultimately you are responsible," says Linda Drake, CEO of TCIM, an information services company focusing on customer care.

Always be prepared for your advisory board meetings to get the most benefit from them. Choose a location for the meeting that is free of distractions. It's a good idea to distribute essential information in advance of the meeting so your board members have time to review it.

After your meetings, keep the lines of communication open with your board members. The fact they've agreed to serve on your board means they care about your success. Keep them updated on your company's progress. "Ideas without action aren't worth much, so you have to make sure you follow up," says Susan Stautberg.

The opportunity to listen, synthesize and learn from outside expert advice can inspire innovation that will accelerate your business growth.

5

DEVELOP THE RIGHT TEAM

ONE OF THE MOST difficult transitions for a growing business is morphing from a fledging startup to a more established, mature organization. Many entrepreneurs who want to grow their firms stumble because they can't adjust their business operations appropriately. I liken it to going through puberty. It can be awkward, confusing, and frustrating, but it's a part of growing up.

One of the biggest areas of change comes in the management of the company. Processes, policies, and procedures must be implemented to ensure success. You may need to make personnel adjustments. One of the first changes that you, as the CEO, need to make is to let go so you can work *on* the business, not *in* the business.

Let Go to Grow

If you are like most entrepreneurs, you think no one in your organization can do the job as well as you can. Candidly, I have a tendency to think that way myself. As my company grew, it was difficult to step aside and let others run with a project. But once I did, it was liberating. If you micromanage, you get bogged down in too many minutiae to execute the strategic vision you have crafted. Your time gets eaten away. The business is driving you, instead of you driving your business. You should put together a crackerjack team of individuals and let them do their thing. Get out of their way. It's time to let go and learn to work on your business, not in the business.

In many respects, delegation is one of the most critical skills you need to achieve personal and professional success as an entrepreneur. There is, however, more to delegation than assigning projects and tasks. It's important to be able to wisely choose which responsibilities to delegate. Take a look at your current work flow and decide what responsibilities to give and which to retain. Sometimes an outside consultant or executive coach can help you make your selections, because they can see things more objectively.

A personal coach helped Sally Hughes, CEO of Caster Connection, Inc., to stay focused on what her role within the company should be. "I was always the top salesperson within my company, and I sort of had to step back from that role. I passed some of my larger customers off to my salespeople so I could concentrate on the strategy and focus of the company," she says.

Vandover CEO Mary Quigg tried to do it all, but eventually realized the smart thing was to hire a chief operations officer. "Over time I've had an open-book management style, and I really expected all the members of my team to make decisions based on the best interest of the business. But as we grew, we outgrew our structure and my competencies, and I made the decision to hire a chief operating officer," she says.

Quigg understands her decision to hire a COO resulted in some turnover in the senior ranks of her management team, but it has resulted in stronger financial controls, improved reporting, better processes, and stronger leadership. It also helped her learn to be a CEO. "We're better positioned for future growth," she notes.

Results are what count most for Melanie Bergeron. "I am really big on the communication part. I explain, here is the plan, and this is what we need to do. Then I tell them what it's going to look like, and if it's not done I want to know why. You can't be someone who is standing right on top of people while they are trying to work. You have to let them do it. Empower them and let them do their work."

Bergeron keeps an agenda for each of her direct reports, so when she meets with them she can keep track of all the projects they are working on and the current status. She advises:

> You have to be a very good listener, and you can't get too caught up on the details. Try to stay a thousand feet above what's going on. A lot of times, ideas and projects will pick up really strong direction, and then other things will come up and those original projects will need to be set on the back burner for a while. We give people the freedom to make mistakes . . . as long as they learn from their mistakes. I think that induces a lot of creativity and leads to people taking more risks.

I agree with Melanie. I believe in giving people the opportunity to fail. That may sound odd, but think of it this way: If someone can't fail, then can they really succeed? When someone understands the impact of their decisions and actions, they take them more seriously. I hate when employees shrug their shoulders and say, "It's not my job." Well, make it their job and allow them to rise to the occasion.

Another policy I instituted in my company is what I call the problem/solution discussion. When someone on the staff comes to me with a problem, they aren't allowed to ask me what I think they should do about it. Rather, they must come prepared with solutions to recommend. This minimizes the time it takes me to make a good decision. Additionally, when they come to me with a work product for approval I ask them, "Is this the very best job you could have possibly done?" It's a waste of everyone's time for me to be correcting spelling errors or catching glitches in video editing. When it gets to my desk, it should be a solid product.

Sheri Orlowitz of Shan Industries believes in consensus management. "I am a very hands-on CEO, but I also believe in delegation," she says. "I expect that the people who work for and with me will help shape the solutions and challenge me. When I go into a meeting to make a decision I have an idea and a direction, but rarely do I come out with my initial solution." Keep in mind you want to spend your time and energy on things that will drive your company forward. Use your time wisely and stay focused on your vision. Let go to grow.

Take Action Every Day

Aerodynamically the bumblebee shouldn't be able to fly, but the bumblebee doesn't know that so it goes on flying anyway.

—Mary Kay Ash

Once you've let go to grow, you need to make a commitment to yourself that you'll take action every day toward your business goals. Don't let a single day pass without doing at least one activity that will help move your business farther. Because if you allow one day to pass, that one day becomes two days, which turn into weeks and then months. Procrastination is your biggest enemy.

Create a reasonable action plan. Then, ask yourself at the beginning of each day, what is the most important thing I can do today to move the business forward. Don't try to accomplish everything all at once. Not only is that impossible, but it will overwhelm you. The most important thing you can do for your business is to keep the ball moving forward. Reward yourself along the way, and don't forget to share successes with your team.

Hire the Right People

You're only as good as the people you hire.

—Ray Kroc

You really have no chance of succeeding in your business without the right team. Your employees are your company, and they can make or break your business over time. A lot of small businesses have a difficult time with the hiring process.

Does the following scenario sound familiar? Your neighbor's cousin Joe just graduated from college and is looking for a job. You are in desperate need of someone to work in your company, so you hire him. Bad decision for a couple of reasons. First, hiring someone for no better reason than they are a warm body rarely works out. You should never permit your business to get into a situation where your back is to the wall and you resort to hiring the first person who walks by. Secondly, hiring family and friends in most cases is a disaster. Not only can it wreak havoc on your business, but it can result in lost friendships and very uncomfortable family events.

Pamela Chambers O'Rourke says she hired a couple of her friends, and it turned out to be a terrible decision. "I had known them for over ten years, and it was hard when I had to let them go, but it was because they were unethical and didn't represent the business in a professional manner—the Icon way. When it comes to money, you have no friends," she warns.

Because people judge a business by its managers and employees, select employees carefully. Your hiring process shouldn't be a "find me somebody now" situation. Instead, it should be a well-managed process that helps you minimize selection mistakes—which is another example of the importance of business planning.

"I surround myself with such smart people. That was a huge growth thing for me. Originally, I hired the type of people that I felt I could afford to do the job to get it done. But to bring the company to an entirely different level, salary-wise, I had to pay more and understand the value of those people," explains Diane Buzzeo, CEO of Marketing Concepts.[1]

While there is no method of hiring that guarantees you'll get it right every time, there are some things you can do to reduce the number of misfits. Keep in mind that in their quest to find the most talented employee, many business owners wind up with the most talented job seeker instead.

Choosing the wrong job applicant can be a costly mistake. According to Carol A. Hacker in *The Costs of Bad Hiring Decisions & How to Avoid Them*,[2] the average cost of a bad hire can be one-third of the annual salary—that's assuming the mistake is discovered and corrected within the first six months the new employee is on the job. That's why it is critical to find people who have the skills and personality traits that are a good fit for the job and your company culture.

The first step in the process is to write a clear, detailed job description. A good job description begins with a careful analysis of the important facts about a job, such as the individual tasks involved, the methods used to complete the tasks, the purpose and responsibilities of the job, the relationship of the job to other positions, and the qualifications needed for the job.

Patricia Whitaker, president of Arcturis, an architectural and design firm, has learned a lot about hiring employees. In twenty-seven years she has seen her firm's staff grow from one to more than seventy employees, and her company has become one of the country's leading design firms.

As with her projects, her approach to hiring new employees starts with a hiring blueprint, which is a list of duties and expectations created before the talent search begins. "We create it before we interview someone and send it to ask them if this job is something they'd be interested in? If we are interested in them, we want them to know what they are getting into before they get here," she explains.[3]

It's also a good idea to get your team involved in the initial screening process of job applicants. Let those who will be working with the new hire narrow the pool of candidates down for management review. Include your team during the interviewing process, too.

From my own personal perspective, I believe the interview is the key to identifying the right individual. It gives you a better sense of the individual and how the candidate will fit into the culture of your organization. It's intuitive with me. If I don't get a good feeling about the person during the interview, I've learned that despite what their qualifications are it's probably not going to work.

"I believe in asking about significant life events," says Marsha Firestone, president of the Women Presidents' Organization. "Ask them what their most significant accomplishment was and what was their most challenging effort. The more detailed of an analysis they provide, the more comfortable I feel."

Always take time to prepare for the interview. Review each candidate's resume and make a list of pertinent questions that apply to the specific job criteria. Of course, you must conduct yourself professionally during the interview and treat all job applicants fairly.

Hire the Best Candidate, Not the Best Job Seeker

Depending on what your business is, you may want to consider using situational interviews. These are interviews that ask a candidate to actually demonstrate how they would handle a specific project or situation. Situational interviews help companies get beyond the resume to capture a truer sense of how an applicant would perform on the job. For example, the situational interview could involve taking a tour of the workplace and asking the interviewee to actually perform some aspect of the job. Of course, such an interview should only be conducted with candidates who are being seriously considered.

According to Iris Salsman, a principal in the public relations firm of Salsman Lundgren Public Relations:

People can stage their qualifications in a way that isn't really an accurate portrayal of how they really are on the job. And, of course, with references they're not going to give us anybody who is going to say anything bad. Plus, people are very careful about what they say.

As Salsman explains, "We ask candidates to do two things. We give them a topic and ask them to write a press release. Then, we walk the candidates through a couple of typical role-playing situations—examples of the kinds of things they'll be confronted with on the job. In our industry, they are going to have to think on their feet, and they have to develop relationships with people that they never see face-to-face, and it gives us a sense of whether or not they can do this."

Research data shows situational interviews are about 50 percent more effective than traditional interviews. However, you must use them carefully. Make sure you advise the candidate in advance about what will be expected. Most likely, the candidates will be nervous, so take time to make them as comfortable as possible. Don't be surprised if you lose a few candidates who are uncomfortable with the process and decide not to go forward.

The framework for the situational interview should closely match the job responsibilities, and you should establish objective criteria for judging each candidate's performance. Make a list of the skills and traits that you believe are essential to the job function. Use your list to evaluate each candidate. Depending on the size of your company, you may want to form an interview team. Team members can then discuss and compare responses based on the job criteria.

As with any hiring process, you must be aware of the legal implications involved. It is a good idea to consult with your company's attorney or with a human resource professional.

Sometimes the best candidate is not the best qualified in terms of formal training. Keep in mind, skills can be taught, but it is difficult to succeed when a person doesn't fit into your culture. So it's just as important to consider whether the individual is a good personality fit. Squeezing a square peg into a round hole not only can bog things down, but can have a significant impact on morale.

"The first step is deciding who the right person is. My partner and I decided early on that we needed to have a clear focus on what qualities we wanted in the individuals we employed to possess," says Rebecca Olson, cofounder of Evolving Solutions, a $45 million company. "We decided we would focus our hiring efforts on individuals who share our beliefs and values in regard to customer service, integrity, responsibility, work ethic, and motivation."[4]

Watch out for glaring red flags. I hired an SBTV.com employee who on paper seemed to be too good to be true. She was immensely qualified, but her resume looked like a catalog of companies. She'd skipped from job to job to job. However, when I inquired about that issue, she seemed to have a plausible explanation. So I ignored her job hopping, my gut instincts and hired her anyway. Well, I soon figured out the reason she couldn't hold a job for very long—she was a real troublemaker. She spent more time trying to create turmoil around the office than doing her job—which, by the way, she wasn't interested in most of the time any way. It was only a few months before she resigned. As far as I know, she works temp jobs now. Geez—I wonder why?

Your goal isn't to simply fill names in the boxes of an organization chart. You are building a team of talented individuals who are as interested in succeeding as you are. These individuals are one of your greatest assets. Choose wisely.

Invest in Retention: Get Started on the Right Foot

Once you have selected the right employee, make sure you employ strategies to motivate and retain that individual. According to PricewaterhouseCoopers' "Saratoga Human Capital Index Report," 46 percent of new hires are gone in the first year.

Because the hiring process is expensive, it's smart to start investing in retention the very first day on the job. Make sure you integrate the new employee into your work force. Don't put them at a desk hoping they'll figure it out from there. The only thing they'll figure out is how to start looking for their next position.

The first day on a new job is much like the first day of school. A new employee is both excited and apprehensive. With that in mind, make the new employee feel comfortable and accepted. You only have one chance to make a good first impression. Employees who have negative initial experiences typically don't stay around for long. That means you're back at square one. So why not take the time to do it right.

Prior to the new employee's first day, mark off sufficient time on your calendar to personally greet the new hire and introduce her to the team. If you aren't going to be available, assign someone within your organization to make sure she isn't left to fend for herself.

Make it a priority at some point during the day to spend time getting to know the new additions to your staff. Ask them about their hobbies and interests and look for common areas of interest. This gives you the opportunity to get to know them on a more personal level.

At the Vandiver Group, when new employees join the company, they are invited to attend a "Koosh Ball" ceremony, where they receive a Koosh Ball to symbolize a spirit of fun and creativity. The ceremony continues with a reading of "Willie Was Different," a Norman Rockwell children's book about the value of diversity and accepting individual differences. "We conclude with a discussion on the culture of the organization and what we look for and honor in ourselves and clients," explains Donna Vandiver.

Consider putting up a welcome banner in the new employees' workspace or giving them a special parking space for the day. Don't stick them in a makeshift work area. Plan ahead and be sure their work space is prepared. They should have the work tools and supplies they need to get started. In addition, provide them with their e-mail address, initial password, and telephone number so they feel as though they are connected. Juliette Douglas of FJ Douglas and

Associates says, "Make sure you have some things in writing for them. They are not going to remember everything. And don't forget some of the basics, like how to use the telephone, and who your clients are, and have that constant feedback. Make sure they understand what is expected, and if you can, watch them do it to make sure they understand."

You might also want to give them a specific assignment—something they can get started on to feel as though they are contributing. Don't forget to provide them with copies of your company's mission statement, and core values.

Touch base with the new employees throughout the day to see how things are going. You want them to feel comfortable asking questions and learning the ropes.

Identify Your Company's Pink Cadillac

The whole idea is to engage people in your mission, make them see things as you do, make them care about it more than anything else.
—Shelly Lazarus, CEO, Ogilvy & Mather Worldwide

Mary Kay Cosmetics was created by one woman, Mary Kay Ash, who had a desire to enrich women's lives. She began by offering cosmetic products to enhance a woman's image and giving women a perfect business opportunity to help them earn extra money, enjoy more flexibility, and grow as independent business owners. More than forty years later, the company has 1.7 million independent consultants, with sales in 2006 of more than $2.25 billion. Part of the company's success are a motivated, committed sales force and the opportunity to drive the coveted pink Cadillac.

So what's your company's pink Cadillac? Having an unmotivated employee on your payroll is the equivalent of spending money on a sleek sports car and putting it in the garage and never driving it. Why bother if you can't get any enjoyment out of it? It's a waste of money. Yet, there are lots of employees who are just going through the motions without caring about, or being engaged in, their work. In fact, 23 percent of workers admitted to looking for a new job on company time, according to research conducted for the staffing firm, Hudson Highland Group. The research also found 39 percent of the workers surveyed classified themselves as trapped—not committed to the organization but planning to stay nonetheless.

To protect your investment in your employees, you need to ensure they are engaged and motivated. So here are some rules to live by:

Make it fun.

Make it creative.

Make it flexible.

Make it rewarding.

Make it empowering.

A lot of small businesses worry they can't retain employees, because they can't compete from a salary and benefits standpoint with big companies who have deep pockets. However, money isn't always the greatest motivator. The majority of people desire recognition for a job well done, and many are willing to work for less money to be part of an organization that gives them an opportunity to excel and grow. A recent study conducted by the Gallup organization found employee recognition was one of the twelve key dimensions of a great workplace. *Harvard Business Review* reported the use of rewards was the single highest predictor of organizational results. According to the U.S. Department of Labor, 46 percent of skilled workers are currently leaving their organizations because they feel unappreciated.

Recognition can be a powerful management tool. If you spend time recognizing the good things employees do, you'll most likely find yourself spending less time on the bad things they do. It's simply human nature. You'll get more of the behavior you reward.

Employee recognition programs don't have to be formalized or expensive. Some companies utilize spot rewards, whereby an employee may receive a gift card to Starbucks or movie tickets. You might consider implementing an Employee of the Month program with special perks. Even something as simple as a pat on the back or a bouquet of balloons can go a long way in motivating employees and increasing loyalty.

"Staff meetings can motivate employees, because they promote communication. Staff meetings are also a good place for public praise and awards," says WPO founder Marsha Firestone.

For rewarding five years of service, Pamela Chambers O'Rourke came up with an interesting recognition. "Women get a Louis Vuitton purse, and men get a choice of a Louis Vuitton wallet or a watch. My turnover is very, very low. How many women do you know who would go out and buy themselves a Louis Vuitton bag? Not me. It's something really special," she says. (I don't know about you, but I wouldn't mind working for Pamela.)

You can engage your employees by allowing them to be informed about company objectives and performance. Your team should understand what the expectations are and how their role in the company can help meet the objectives. And every employee should feel as though they have a voice.

"Always treat people the way you want to be treated. Just remember to thank people. Ask for advice, and when you do, listen. When you listen and treat people with respect, they are going to bend over backwards to help you in so many ways," says Melanie Bergeron.

Avis Yates Rivers, CEO of Technology Concepts, says she likes to give her employees a sense of ownership. "I always let them know I will support them, whatever decisions they make, even if it turns out to be the wrong decision. I'd rather they make a decision as opposed to doing nothing."

Attract the Best and the Brightest Through Innovation and Creativity

It is often difficult for small companies to compete head to head with major corporations when providing fringe benefits, such as health-care coverage, tuition reimbursement programs, or matching 401(k) plans. As a woman-owned growing enterprise, you do have one huge advantage. You can create a company culture and environment that attracts the best and the brightest by embracing creativity and engaging employee innovation.

Companies that inspire and value innovation and creativity are great places to work. Too many big companies shut down creativity within the organization. How many people do you know who work in huge companies who are miserable? They complain about the pressure. They hate their bosses. They particularly hate the same-old, same-old routine. As Michael Gerber likes to say, "They are just doing it, doing it, doing it." There's no meaning or purpose.

Take a look around your office. Does it inspire creative thinking? Is it a boring, white space? Think about Google's offices. Employees there have access to a fitness center, massages, any type of food cooked to order, and a video game room. Okay, I know that's a little over the top, but you can create a fun environment. In the recreation area of my offices, we have purple laminated kitchen cabinets with brushed silver countertops. In the main office area you'll find a few bright red walls with splashes of purple here and there. Not too crazy, but interesting enough to add some flair.

Now ask yourself this question. Do you find yourself shutting down an idea because you've never done it that way? Welcome new ideas and give employees the opportunity to try innovative things. Dedicate time to brainstorming sessions, or hire a creativity consultant to stimulate innovative thinking within your organization.

Make your company a fun place to work. Employees should look forward to coming to work every day, rather than being stressed out and on the edge of burnout all the time. At SBTV.com, we have a dog-friendly office. I'm often greeted in the morning with a sloppy kiss from one of our four-legged team members. Of course, I'm sure the fact I keep dog treats in my desk has nothing to do with my popularity. The dogs create a playful environment and go a long way toward alleviating stress. Plus, our employees enjoy having their "best friend" nearby.

Dancing Deer Baking Company founder and CEO Trish Karter's motto is, "When people aren't happy, it shows in the food, and in every other aspect of the business." Therefore, "we spent a lot of energy early on trying to figure out how to create an organization that has happy people in it."

At Adesso Lighting, everyone tries to maintain a good sense of humor. "From the very beginning, we wanted to build the kind of company that provides a very friendly, relaxed kind of atmosphere, where people take their jobs very seriously but do not take themselves so seriously," says owner Peggy Traub.

Imagine six weeks of additional vacation with pay after six years of service. Melanie Bergeron offers a six-week sabbatical program at Two Men and a Truck. Not only is the program a great employee benefit, but it also helps the company. She says that "it helps us cross-train people to do other jobs in their department. When the employee on sabbatical comes back, there is a big bouquet of flowers on their desk, and their e-mails are cleared out and they are starting fresh. People take these sabbaticals for weddings, surgeries, and even to participate in Peace Corps activities."

Maintaining an engaged and motivated workforce and creating an environment where people really want to work is one important characteristic of truly successful companies.

Take Emotions Out of the Workplace

Many women business owners, as they grow their businesses, find the team they started with may not have the skills necessary to fit with a larger enterprise. Because these individuals have been there from day one, they can't let them go. As a result, they postpone making critical personnel decisions, or they won't relocate their business because they worry a relocation or a merger with another company might mean losing some of the staff. You shouldn't be callous or arbitrary when it comes to personnel decisions, but you need to make business decisions based on what is best overall for the company. Consequently, you can't let emotions dictate your decisions.

If putting the personal stuff aside is difficult for you, find someone to act as the go-between. In my company, my partner, Michael Kelley, handles most of the personnel issues, and he is very skilled at it. Of course, the three of us (Dan Demko, Michael, and I) discuss everything, but Michael is the one who ultimately does the hiring, firing, and disciplining.

Using an outside human resource firm can also be a good way to manage your staff. In addition to taking some of the responsibility off your plate, they can make sure you handle personnel issues legally so you won't wind up in court.

As your company grows it's also necessary to create employee manuals to ensure you are treating each employee equally and fairly. These policies should be communicated to your entire staff and should cover things such as sick days, holidays and vacation days. Language about discrimination and harassment should also be included. There are a lot of off-the-shelf manuals available, but I don't recommend them.

A good place to start for information and assistance is the EEOC—Equal Employment Opportunity Council (www.eeoc.gov). The laws governing employee relations are complex. There are federal employment laws, and each state also has it own unique laws which can vary greatly. Plus, certain industries, such as health care and transportation, have special considerations. My best advice is to consult with a human resource professional and/or an attorney who specializes in employment law. Don't wait until it's too late.

Tap into Hidden Talents

When you hire an employee, you focus on the skills that are necessary for a particular job. From then on, that's the way you think of that particular employee. However, employees often have hidden talents that could help you take your business to the next level. You need to take the time to discover these hidden treasures. That means you'll have to do a little digging. Once uncovered, however, if you can match those special skills and hidden talents with the right position, you'll have a match made in heaven. Your company will benefit, and the employee will excel.

Employees who identify their talents and passions and apply those toward driving the business usually do much better. Asking your staff about their strengths and passions is a great way to create a motivated workforce. Small meetings often provide an opportunity to ascertain valuable information about what drives employees and how those talents can be used to grow the company. Employee outings can also reveal some unique characteristics. Play time is a good time to discover an employee's hidden talent. Schedule a company softball game and picnic or consider planning a company talent show. Informal, fun environments provide a safe way for employees to showcase their talents with an added benefit of enhancing employee morale.

Outside consultants and/or coaches are helpful in designing activities and exercises to uncover special skills. Plus, employees often feel more comfortable with someone from outside the company.

Once you have identified an employee's talents and passions, develop a plan to incorporate them into her job responsibilities. If this means additional training or experience for her, it's an excellent investment.

"I have always had a philosophy of allowing employees to take classes in anything they want to learn, given budget constraints and time with the company, and so on. Most people, especially star performers, will pay back in performance any money that is ever invested in them. I let them pick any classes—even art and music. Goals and dream development are a constant process," says Trish McCarty, president and founder of Education Resources/StarShine Academy.

"Developing employees is just as important as growing sales. It's also important to me that my employees are happy and love coming into work and are committed to working here for a long time," says Peggy Traub.

Small businesses need to utilize every resource to the fullest. Discovering hidden employee talents can be a big boost to your bottom line.

Create Systems to Ensure Consistent Results

Businesses that grow to multimillion-dollar enterprises develop systems which can be replicated time and time again. Many entrepreneurs suffer from process phobia. But that's no way to run a successful growth enterprise. You need to have an analytical approach to the delivery of your product or service. In order to ensure consistent results, you must create systems and practices. If you are in manufacturing, that probably seems intuitively obvious. You have to create the same product with the same specs over and over again. Regardless of what business you are in, your customers or clients expect consistent results, and that means systematic and scalable delivery.

Without process, things can easily slip through the cracks. Someone passes an aspect of a project off to someone else and assumes it will be handled appropriately. Later, and often too late, you learn that it not only wasn't handled correctly, it wasn't handled at all. Inconsistent results can put you out of business. The bigger your company gets, the more important is process." During the 1980s, we were experiencing exploding growth, but we did not have the proper systems in place to handle it, which almost overwhelmed the business. We simply could not keep up with the demand for our products. We had a huge backlog of unshipped orders. It was the one time where we were in danger of going into bankruptcy, but luckily, I secured a last minute loan from my bank, and we worked 24 hours a day, seven days a week, to ship out our customer orders in time for the Christmas holiday," explained mail-order catalog pioneer, Lillian Vernon.[5]

Peggy Mitchusson of The Face and The Body has taken great pains over the years to hone her processes to create a standard that will ensure the most predictable outcome for her clients. With 165 employees, it starts with her training process. For instance, every step of a facial is spelled out in clinical terms so everyone administering a facial knows exactly what the procedure should be and even how long each step should take. This ensures every client is getting the same treatment and knows what to expect every time. Peggy says if she gets negative feedback from a customer, it can usually be traced back to one of the steps not being followed. The language of her "service menu" is written with the client in mind:

> Whatever the treatment is going to consist of, and whatever the promise is, including the amount of time it takes, is spelled out so the customer knows exactly what to expect.

When you take the time to write down business procedures and policies, you are creating a vehicle for smooth operational transitions from one employee to another. It also allows you to step away from the day-to-day operational details. Such documentation may be the most important asset your company owns.

Learn from Resignations to Help You Grow

No matter how hard you try to build great company, not every employee is going to want to stay. When an employee decides to leave your organization it's unsettling. Typically they give you the standard reasons of "better pay" or "better opportunity." But neither may be the real reason for their departure. According to Leigh Branham, author of 7 *Hidden Reasons Why Employees Leave*, more than 80 percent of employees don't leave because the grass is greener on the other side of the fence. Instead, it's because of negative factors in the workplace. Learning from resignations can help you enhance your company operations for growth.

Employee turnover is expensive. Furthermore, an employee's resignation can have an impact on the morale and productivity of your remaining staff. As a smart business owner you owe it to the health of your business to examine the true motivation of an employee's departure by conducting an exit interview.

Exit interviews can be eye opening. They provide an opportunity to gather information about your company that might otherwise be difficult to obtain while someone is working for you. The interview may cover issues such as benefits, working conditions, opportunities for career advancement, the quality and quantity of the workload, and relationships with coworkers and supervisors.

"The goal of the exit interview is to learn about your company's culture, your hiring practices and your review practices. You want to know the areas where you need to improve," says Mary Quigg, CEO of Vandover.

To conduct a successful exit interview, set aside about half an hour in a quiet, private area. Because it's difficult to conduct an exit interview, carefully plan ahead what questions you intend to ask and what information you'd like to obtain. Start off by trying to gain the trust of the departing employee and control the conversation so it doesn't become confrontational. Some questions you might consider asking are:

1. Why are you leaving?

2. How would you suggest we train your replacement?

3. What were the most challenging issues in your job?

4. How would you improve job satisfaction here?

5. What did you like most about your job?

6. Were you happy with the pay and benefits?

7. How do you feel the business is run?

8. Were there any policies that made your job more difficult?

9. Would you recommend working for this business to friends? Why/Why not?

10. What did you dislike most about your job?

If the employee is a valuable part of your team, be sure to ask if there is anything you can do to make her want to stay. You might be surprised by what you learn, and the entire conversation may turn into a negotiation. For example, suppose an employee is leaving because she wants to be able to work from home, but she's afraid it won't be acceptable. You may be able to arrange a schedule that works for both of you and the employee will be saved. However, as Quigg notes:

> By the time someone has made the decision to resign, it is probably too late to do anything about it, because that's a really big decision. What you can do is learn what you could have done differently, so you can keep from losing other employees for similar reasons.

If you aren't comfortable doing the exit interview yourself, or if you don't think the employee will be honest with you, consider using an outside human resources professional. In fact, many small companies find this is actually more productive. Small business owners typically have close relationships with their employees. As a result, the employee is often more comfortable being honest with someone from outside the firm. In fact, small business owners probably shouldn't conduct exit interviews of their direct reports. They most likely will fill freer to express their opinions when talking with a third-party.

IMPLEMENT KEY
MARKETING STRATEGIES

NOTHING HAPPENS until you sell something. So it should go without saying that every business needs a marketing plan. There are great resources that can help you draft a solid marketing plan. (Check some of the resources listed in Chapter 10.) This chapter is not intended to provide a course in Marketing 101. Instead, my goal is to help you identify and implement key marketing strategies to help grow your business.

Create a Killer Brand

Brands, like countries, have their own cultures, traditions, and languages.
—Maxine Clark, founder, Build-A-Bear Workshop

Did you know the average American mentions specific brands fifty-six times a week in conversation, according to market researcher

Keller Fay Group. Your mission—should you decide to accept it—is to make sure one of those brands is yours.

In order to develop your company's brand, go back to your vision, mission, and value statements. These should be the foundation of your marketing plan, because they state where you are headed, what your core business is, and what value you deliver to your customers and employees.

Then take a long hard look at your current branding. Does it project the image you want for your business? Your brand should be designed to create the buzz that will get your business noticed. A well-crafted brand often becomes synonymous with the product or service offering. Think Starbucks—and you think high-end, quality coffee drinks. Think Midas and you automatically think mufflers. Kleenex is the term often used for a facial tissue.

"Branding is creating an image and awareness and a presence of who you are so people hopefully will seek you out for what you have to offer. It's your promise. It's your positioning. And it's your personality," explains Michele Lando, president of Skill Set Communications.

Your brand is more than your logo, business card, and letterhead. It penetrates every aspect of your company, from your office location, to how your phone is answered, to how you present yourself, to the final delivery of your product or service. You can spend thousands of dollars on a marketing campaign touting your company's great customer service, but consistently rude employees will defeat your efforts.

For example, my mother had to be placed in a skilled nursing facility a number of years ago. Several places were recommended to us, but the one my dad and I chose sent us a beautiful four-color brochure that touted the virtues of their friendly staff and showed pictures of nicely decorated rooms with comfortable couches and chairs. When we arrived, the room was barren—nothing but an uncomfortable hospital bed—and the staff was at their very best indifferent. Dad and I were furious. We had been completely misled. Mom spent only one night there because we moved her to another location the very next day.

To make sure the essence of your brand is being communicated at all levels, step back and experience your business the way your customers and clients do. For example, try calling your office sometime to see how your phone is being answered, but make sure caller ID doesn't identify the boss is calling. Is it an experience that would make someone feel welcomed, or does the person on the other end sound preoccupied and uninterested?

In 2005, Mary Quigg recognized she needed to reevaluate her company's branding. She understands that a strong brand and consistent messaging have contributed to both client retention and successful word of mouth marketing. She says:

> As a business owner, it can be easy to consider "branding" a luxury and put it off until you have "extra" dollars. Over time, I've come to realize it is a necessity and a worthwhile investment—and always a work in progress. In addition to using outside resources, our internal marketing and communications staff devote much of their time making sure all of our messages remain consistent to our brand.

Sometimes the little things are just as important for your branding efforts as the big things. For example, when Dany Levy launched DailyCandy.com she placed postcards in restaurants as a form of grassroots marketing, but she stopped short of placing them on car windshields when a friend insisted it didn't seem appropriate for a brand focused on fashion and lifestyle.

Similarly, Melanie Sabelhaus, founder of Exclusive Interim Properties (EIP), knew the high-end executive clients she was trying to attract to her corporate housing business were used to the finest quality. Therefore, even though she was just starting out, she furnished her corporate apartments with fine crystal, china, and linens. Impressive—you bet. Little did her clients know the finery came from a retail discounter.

Finally, don't forget about you. As the CEO, you are the primary spokesperson for the company. Your employees, customers, suppliers, and other stakeholders all look to you to personify your brand. As Michele Lando notes:

> Branding is your life. It's not a question of whether or not you will be a brand, you are a brand. The question is whether you will be a brand by design, or be a brand by default. Your brand is actually built from the inside out. It is the essence of who you are. It is your values and your belief systems and how you express them.

Everywhere you go, everything you do, and everything your employees do, says something about your company and its brand.

Shake Things Up: Create a Unique Value Proposition

Doing business the same old way, day in and day out—maintaining the status quo—equates to nothing more than a mediocre business. In today's competitive environment, you must continually reevaluate your business. Successful businesses shake things up.

Million-dollar women business owners are leaders, not followers. They see the world differently. Their businesses flourish because they identify unique market opportunities and deliver products and services in a unique way. They are innovators and inventors who are transforming the world with new ideas. One would never describe their enterprises as the same old same old. They fill market voids and continually strive to find better and better delivery processes. Innovation, creativity, and imagination in products and services are requirements to excel in business today.

"I asked our membership if they could identify the one best strategy that was the most indicative of whether or not a business would succeed, and overwhelmingly the response was innovation. These women have such creative products that they were able to be unique in the marketplace," says Marsha Firestone, president of the Women Presidents' Organization.

Similarly, we polled our SBTV.com audience and asked them what was the most important ingredient for business success, and the answer was "a killer idea."

After having worked in a variety of areas in the retail industry, Adesso Lighting founder Peggy Traub realized there was an enormous niche opportunity in contemporary, but affordable, lighting.

"I had been a Bloomingdale's lighting buyer and I knew there was great contemporary lighting coming out of Italy that retailed for $200 to $800 dollars. There also was an abundance of lamps in the $30 to $150 price range, but they were very traditional brass, crystal, and ceramic. There was nothing for a moderate budget in the contemporary category. I saw a real opportunity to create contemporary lighting that would be affordable to people who had the same kind of budget as somebody buying more traditional lamps," she explains.

In 1994, she and her new partner, Lee Schaak, traveled to Taiwan and developed their first line. They returned to New York, found office space, and started drafting a business plan. "We managed to get space at the largest furniture industry trade show. We didn't have any advance notice, so Lee scrounged around at Home Depot and managed overnight to put together our new exhibit space—even pulling a couple of chairs out of the trash to sit on. And we have been innovating ever since."

In addition to a unique product strategy, Peggy's company started with a philosophy to do things differently in the industry. "We made a commitment to rethink industry practices: We did unique things, like putting a service card in every carton, thanking the customer for buying an Adesso product and offering an 800 number for questions or problems. We also committed to shipping each lamp base and shade in a single box, thereby improving shipping costs and customer service. From the beginning we did things that were smarter than our competition, both in terms of the design and operations, and our sales growth showed the results," she says.

Another successful woman entrepreneur launched a business focusing on women's feet. We all know that women's shoes are designed for appearance, not to be comfortable or practical. And I think most of you would agree that they can be downright painful at times. After years of jamming our feet into pointed toes and balancing on stilettos, our feet pay the price. Orthopedic surgeon Taryn Rose understands that better than most. And she decided to do something about it.

"I saw a lot of women who needed help, whether it be surgery or just better shoes," Taryn says. "But comfortable, fashionable footwear really didn't exist. I did a lot of research on how to make footwear while I was still in medicine. Finally, I decided that I was going to commit fully to my idea. I created footwear that was comfortable, but very fashionable and luxurious for women who want to wear designer clothes but need shoes that can keep up with their busy lifestyle. My shoes now sell in Beverly Hills, Harrods of London, and will be opening in Korea soon."

Square One Organic Vodka founder Allison Evanow identified a unique value proposition when she saw a print ad for a non-organic vodka that bragged about how pure it was based on the number of times it was distilled using fancy filtration methods. "I found it odd that so many vodka brands were more concerned with 'cleaning up' the vodka during the back end of the process, instead of starting with the purest ingredients available," she says.

After researching the idea, she noticed there were only a few organic spirits in the marketplace and that nobody had yet seemed to create the benchmark for the best organic vodka. Furthermore, she felt that just being organic on the inside was not enough, and she thought an organic spirits company that took a holistic approach to the environment was a great opportunity to tackle an untapped niche in a very profitable category.

Creating new products is not the only way to innovate and shake up the market. Sometimes simply repackaging a product offering can be more appealing to your customers. New distribution tactics and a revamped sales strategy are also both excellent ways to be innovative. Sometimes innovation requires a fresh approach to your customer relationships.

One of Patty Briguglio's clients at MMI Associates, Lana Calloway, owns Exhibit Resources, a full-service exhibit design agency. "Lana's business has thrived in a tough market because of the additional value she brings. She developed a rental program for clients that enables them to participate in major trade shows at a fraction of the cost of purchasing major exhibit properties. She rents high-end exhibit properties to clients, making minor modifications to fit their individual needs. This fresh approach allows budget efficiencies for clients and creates new revenue for Exhibit Resources," Briguglio explains.

When you shake things up and create a unique value proposition, you give your potential customers and clients a reason to change their habits. Remember human beings are creatures of habits, and if someone has been purchasing a particular product or service from one company and they are satisfied with that service why should they make a change? The only reason to change to your product is because you offer something better that makes their lives easier. Complete this sentence:

If everyone did business with you, the world would be a better place because . . .

Cultivate and Connect with Customers and Clients

It's easier and less costly to keep an existing client than it is to get a new one. Million-dollar women business owners know 80 percent of their business comes from 20 percent of their customers. So cultivating and connecting with customers and clients to build a loyal customer base is imperative for a growing business.

The first step in building a loyal customer base is to create realistic expectations and always, always live up to or exceed them. In other words, whatever your value proposition to your customer base—service, price, quality, rapid delivery—you must constantly meet or exceed their needs. Remember, you are only as good as your last sale, and bad news travels fast.

"My own business style is to under promise and over deliver, especially where we are operating lean against companies with big money. It makes us look better when we can say we exceeded our goals," says Allison Evanow, Square One Organic Vodka.

Customer service is the lifeblood of a successful organization. To ensure her company is excelling in that area, APCO's Margery Kraus asks for customer feedback. She strives for a 95-percent satisfaction ratio. "An easy way to stay in touch is to survey your client/customer base. Use those survey results to gauge how well you are doing and make any necessary adjustments," she says.

APCO does such an excellent job of customer service that 70 percent of its business comes from referrals. "Our job is to find solutions. From the very beginning, we got a lot of client feedback saying we were really different. We were adding value to what they did, and they were going to tell other people," Kraus adds.

There is probably no industry as personal and yet competitive as the spa industry. The Face and The Body's founder and CEO, Peggy Mitchusson, knows this better than anyone:

> Our clients are like an informal advisory board. We regularly conduct client surveys to make sure every step of the experience is handled properly. We want to make sure that everything we promise in every facial is followed. We let our employees know this is what we promised and here are the fifteen steps. Typically, when we get something back on a survey it's because one of the steps wasn't followed.

Listening is one of the things Terri Hall says has made her company, DoubleTake Studios, successful. "When we go out and talk with a client or a prospect, we really take into consideration what they are asking, or what goals they want to achieve. We are able to translate that into a project and hopefully end up with something that is going to be very successful for them in the end," she says.

Develop true relationships with your customers. Know more about them than just their name and title. Learn about their families and their personal interests. Beth Bronfman, managing partner of Leibler Bronfman Lubalin, a New York-based, full-service advertising agency, believes that you must make your client your partner and always maintain a trusting relationship.

Keep communication lines open. It's better to address a problem immediately before it escalates into a major blow up. Instill the importance of customer service into every employee, from the person who answers the phone to the top levels of management.

Create a Customer Advisory Board

Creating a customer advisory board is one way to help you keep in touch with your clients' expectations, which can give you a real competitive advantage. Not only does it help you continue to offer what the market wants, it also shows you how your customers feel and lets customers know you want to hear their opinions. In turn, your customers will have a vested interest in your success.

Mary Quigg established a customer advisory committee for Vandover and says a huge benefit occurred during the very first meeting. "One of our clients, who provides a comprehensive best practices relocation benefit, made the statement: 'Vandover's services amount to 2 percent of my overall relocation budget. This 2 percent is the difference between a great relocation program and a world-class relocation program.' His comment was repeated by other members, and 'the 2 percent difference' has been used as an effective marketing theme for us. Certain clients expanded their benefit levels as they learned more about our service offerings. This cross-selling of our services among our clients was an unexpected—and valuable—by-product of our meetings."

The frequency of customer advisory council meetings ranges from twice a year to every eighteen months. It's a good idea to hold the meetings offsite. Typically, committee members aren't paid; however, expenses should be covered. A "thank you" gift is also a nice gesture. Some companies make a donation to a favorite charity. A gift card to a restaurant would also be a good idea. Make sure you have an agenda to keep the meeting moving forward. And some experts suggest investing in a facilitator. This will ensure you get the most objective and unbiased information. Often panelists will not feel free to be open and honest if the business owner or a company executive is in charge of the meeting. Don't turn your customer advisory meeting into a special sales event or try to introduce new products. The panel is there to give you feedback and insight into your business, your market, and important customer issues. Your job is to listen.

Know Your Competition

It's important to get to know your customers, but it is equally important to know your competitors. You may be able to grow your business to a certain level with only a vague understanding of the competitive environment. But a successful, fast-growth company must clearly understand who its primary competitors are and know how to differentiate itself from the pack.

Every business has competitors. That's true even if you think you are in an entirely new market. Think of it this way: There's only so much money to spend in particular markets. Even if you think you don't have a direct competitor, focus on who competes for that money.

Because SBTV.com is the first—and only—video news and information site for small businesses, it might appear as though we have no competitors. But there are all types of media that compete for the same advertising dollars we attract. They might not be in exactly the same business, but we compete with them for a share of the purse.

So you need to really get to know your competitors. You need to know what their strengths and weaknesses are. What is the strategic direction of their company? Who are their suppliers and their major customers? What is their pricing structure?

Over 66 percent of respondents to a survey conducted by the Society of Competitive Intelligence Professionals said competitive intelligence is "extremely" or "very" effective in helping identify market opportunities. Nearly 44 percent found it extremely or very effective in terms of understanding customer demand. Nothing can be more disastrous for a small company than to be blindsided by a competitor's strategy.

As you develop your marketing plan, you should conduct research that will help you gain insight into the competitive landscape. The good news is that competitive research doesn't have to cost a fortune; there are low-cost methods to gather competitive intelligence for your business.

Start by exploring the Internet. Go to one of the search engines and conduct a search. You may discover a lot of helpful information. For example, you may learn about your competitor's personnel changes, a new product offering, or even about lost or new clients.

If your competitors have a website, spend some time there. Websites are a good source of information about a company. Typically, there are backgrounds on the company's management team, along with a history of the company and its mission statement. Some websites also maintain a list of clients. If it's an e-commerce site, you can compare price structures.

Contact your industry trade association. Many small businesses belong to trade associations that provide current research findings. These studies focus on consumers' perceptions of your product or service and growing trends within your industry. Most of these studies are free to association members.

Talk to vendors. One of the best sources of information is vendors. A supplier who also sells to your competitor may be able to share insight about what your competition is up to. Be careful, however. If a supplier discloses information to you, you can safely assume he is doing the same thing with your competitors.

Pay attention to your competitor's advertisements. How are they positioning themselves? How often do they advertise? Where are they advertising? Who are the targets of their ads? Collecting this information will help you get a better understanding of your competitors' strategy in the market.

Don't forget about secret shoppers. Secret shoppers can be a good way to learn about the competition's sales process. Ask a friend or family member to pose as a potential customer and either call your competitor or visit their retail location. Of course, this wouldn't be appropriate if you are in an industry where every sales presentation is customized.

Reach out to business associates to learn more about the marketplace. Chances are there are people within your network who have done business with your competitors. Find out what they liked and what they didn't like.

Competitive intelligence should be an ongoing part of your company's marketing efforts. However, whatever information you obtain, use it constructively to assist your firm's growth. And if you gain access to information that appears to be proprietary, destroy it immediately.

Touch Your Customers in Unique Ways

Consumers are bombarded with advertisements. It's hard to escape the messages trying to get you to buy, buy, buy. As a result, we've become desensitized to much of the advertising swirling around us, and we tune it out, turn it off, or zap it out.

Advertisers are searching for innovative ways to reach a targeted audience with measurable results. Smart companies are identifying methods to reach consumers in very different and unique ways, which allow their message to stand out.

For example, it was the holiday season, and I was flying to San Francisco. Once airborne, the flight attendants began preparing for their usual service, with one exception. They announced a holiday gift would be distributed courtesy of a credit card company. It consisted of a clear quart-sized travel bag, which meets the TSA's standards for carry-on liquids; it also included a toothbrush, toothpaste, and some lotion. What a great idea! A captive audience getting a gift with an advertising message. Then, lunch was served in first class, and on my tray was an advertisement for a GPS system from a leading rental car company. Okay—I get it. We were a captive audience of frequent travelers in first class, who probably rent automobiles on a regular basis. Pretty smart.

The old economy marketing methods that include mass media advertising can be expensive, and they aren't as effective as they once were. In order to accelerate the growth of your company, you need to think outside the box. (I really hate that phrase, but sometimes it says it all.) Where are your customers? How do they get their information?

A veteran teacher, Julia Rhodes got her start in business when her son asked for a dry-erase marker with an eraser on the end. Rhodes learned there wasn't a product like that so she created one and took it to market. However, her finances were used up creating molds and prototypes, which left little for marketing. As a teacher, Rhodes had learned to be creative and resourceful, and so she used her skills to design an unforgettable marketing campaign which landed her a spot on the Jay Leno show.

"I became a walking trade show booth. To free up my hands so I could demonstrate my product, I created white board clothing and I would write and erase on myself. People would ask me where they could get the clothes. I'd say 'No, I make erasers!' But it was a way to market so people would remember me." As she explained, "When I followed up they'd say, 'Oh the eraser gal. I remember you.'"

Small companies spend about $30 billion annually on advertising, according to market-research firm Kelsey Group mostly focused on local newspapers, community publications, and the yellow pages. A lot of innovative entrepreneurs are turning to the Web for targeted, measurable marketing opportunities.

For example, more small businesses are taking advantage of free listings on Craigslist. Andre Lawson Grey, a 47-year old San Francisco resident, uses Craigslist to promote her painting and dry wall company. "Craigslist represents 75 percent of my business. It seems to give me enough contacts that I don't need to do anything else," she says.[1]

Blogs are definitely hot now too. In fact, Scott Ginsberg, whose company is literally called "Hello, my name is Scott," says in his new book, *How to Be That Guy*, if you don't have a blog, you're a putz. Blogs can be an effective and inexpensive communication tool. It's kind of like a journal which you keep on the Web and which represents you and your company's personality.

Your company's blog can serve as a public forum for discussion about new and current products or services, company news and events. Use your blog to position yourself as an expert and your company as a leader in your industry. Managed appropriately, your blog can build trust with your readers, stop false rumors, respond honestly to criticism and nip a public relations crisis in the bud before it can spiral out of control.

"At MMI Associates, we not only blog about what we are doing, but about what our clients are doing. Our clients love reading about themselves, as well as other MMI clients. We try to make the blog humorous and informative, with plenty of hot links embedded in the text to interest readers in clicking on our clients' websites, or to provide them with other important information. Often we invite clients to be guest bloggers on our site. The MMI blog has become an entertaining and instructive daily stop for many people in the Raleigh-Durham area of North Carolina, who want to know 'who's who' and 'what's happening,'" explains Patty Briguglio, CEO of MMI Associates.

Blogs can be an important aspect of your marketing mix, but they must be well cared for. You have to make a commitment to keep content fresh in order to give your audience a reason to return time and time again. The more relevant content you add for your audience, the more traffic you'll generate. Focus on providing resources for your readers, too. Each of your postings should have at least one link to another blog or website.

Text messaging is another clever idea. Steven Kelley started a text messaging service called MESSAGEbuzz. It gives customers a way to communicate a short message to a large group of people very quickly anytime/anywhere. "I call myself the modern day pony express," he quips.

Clients utilize MESSAGEbuzz for such things as mobile advertising, loyalty programs and mobile sweepstakes. Wyndham Hotels & Vacation Resorts uses the service to let fans text-to-win at professional basketball games, such as the Portland Trail Blazers. The University of Southern California uses it to engage students' scavenger hunts and communication of university announcements.

Many companies are starting to use text messages in conjunction with traditional advertising campaigns. For example, you may see a magazine advertisement with a text message code to get more information. Other businesses are asking customers to opt-in so they can text-message special promotional announcements and coupons.

Some of the marketing tricks being used today are pretty far out. You have to be careful that whatever you choose doesn't backfire, as did the marketing campaign for a Turner Broadcasting animated television show that triggered a bomb scare that virtually shut down the city of Boston for a while. Or there's the woman who offered to have a message displayed on her pregnant stomach for the Super Bowl.

Finally, keep in mind, that while some of these ideas are working today, they could easily be old news tomorrow. So think creatively and continually search for new and targeted ways to reach your market.

Become a Media Maven

Ever notice how some companies seem to naturally attract positive media coverage? Do you wonder how they do it? I'll tell you. They understand how to work with the media.

Positive media coverage can catapult your business to a new level. A well-placed quote or feature story is more valuable to your company than an advertisement, and much more cost effective.

To create a media strategy for your company, you need a media plan. Here are guidelines to help you develop a media plan for your company:

Media Plan Guidelines

1. Define your objectives.

2. Define your target audience.

3. Create a timeline.

4. Create a strategy that is unique and newsworthy.

5. Identify resources. Manage in-house or outsource.

6. Identify appropriate media outlets.

7. Develop relationships with the appropriate media contacts.

8. Set goals and measurements for effectiveness.

9. Post releases on your website.

10. Be available.

Start by deciding what your objectives are. Do you want to build brand awareness? Are you trying to educate the market about a product or service? Do you want to become a subject matter expert?

Once you understand what your goals are you can develop your strategy. Journalists are only interested in stories that are compelling to their audience. You don't want to make the mistake of wasting a journalist's time. There are some companies who subscribe to the theory that if they send out enough press releases someone will pick it up. The problem is that journalists who are bombarded with inappropriate material will soon tune you out completely. PR agencies sometimes send our editors at SBTV.com multiple releases that have nothing to do with small business. As a result, their e-mail gets deleted because it's considered irrelevant. The unfortunate thing is that one of their client's might be a good fit for us, but it's too tough to weed through all the garbage.

Make a list of the media you want to target based on their coverage areas. There are online resources that can help you build your media list, such as Bacon's MediaSource and Gebbie Press. These resources also provide preferred contact information. For example, some reporters prefer e-mail as their only form of contact, and they don't want phone calls. Respect their wishes.

Before you approach any of the media outlets, you need to find the right angle. How will you make the story interesting to attract a reporter's attention? Your story idea must be newsworthy, not a promotion for your company, and it needs to be interesting to the audience. If you are targeting television stations, explain what visuals are available. Here are some ideas to help you develop your story:

➤ Tie your story to a timely news event or holiday.

➤ Conduct independent research.

➤ Look for an unusual aspect about your business.

➤ Provide educational information the audience needs to know.

Lots of business owners e-mail or call requesting an interview or feature story on their business because they started small and have grown their business to a thriving enterprise. My response—so what? There are hundreds and hundreds of inspirational stories about successful businesses. To successfully pitch your story you should focus on what makes your business unique. What could a viewer learn from your experience? What special information can you share? It is not the journalist's job to try to figure that out.

"When I look into covering a story, the first thing I look for is how many people it affects. Will this story touch my audience? It doesn't matter who the audience is; if the story doesn't mean something to them as a whole, then it's not worth covering. For example, a vacant house fire doesn't mean anything to most people, but the possibility of a tax hike definitely affects the masses," explains Stephanie Zoller, who produces the news for an NBC affiliate.

Once you have decided on the story you want to tell, draft a media release. Keep in mind, a media release isn't an advertisement. Your first paragraph should answer the questions—who, what, when, where, how, and why. The entire release shouldn't be more than a page and a half.

In some instances, a pitch letter works better than a media release. A pitch letter should be brief and to the point. It establishes what the situation is, who the audience is, why the audience will be interested, and most importantly why you are the best person to interview for the story.

Post your media releases on your website in an easy to access area. Remember, journalists live and die by their deadlines, so make it easy for them to find what they are looking for.

CareerBuilder.com is masterful when it comes to the art of media. Take a look at the press room on their website. There are numerous releases based on their independent research about the impact of timely issues on the hiring market. It's a journalist's dream.

It's important personally to follow up to see if the journalist received your information and to determine the level of interest. Don't be surprised if you have to resend the material. If the journalist accepts phone calls, be respectful of his time and always ask whether he is working on deadline. If the answer is yes, find a good time to call back. On the other hand, if the answer is no, be prepared to quickly and succinctly pitch your story. Don't forget, if the reporter isn't interested, find out what types of stories would be of interest. Don't try to force the issue. Make yourself a welcomed resource, not a pest.

A good salesperson knows: The key to success is listening and understanding what the customer wants. The same is true when you are working with the media. If you consistently work to build those relationships in the right way, your company can become a media magnet, too.

Apply for Awards

There are many awards which can garner valuable attention and visibility for your company. Take advantage of them to put the spotlight on your business.

There's an old saying in marketing: Perception is reality. Awards create credibility for your firm and can assist with your marketing efforts. If you want to grow your business, you want to look as big and successful as you can. Recognition by a third-party speaks volumes. When potential customers and clients read about your company's recognition, it instills confidence in your firm.

In order to be successful, you need to tell your firm's story in an engaging and compelling way. If you aren't a good writer, hire someone to help you. The same is true for your bio. As the CEO and spokesperson for the company, your bio should be written so as to best convey your accomplishments and leadership ability. There are awards presented by your local chamber of commerce; local, state, and federal governments; newspapers and magazines; private companies; and trade associations. Check out the criteria for various awards and apply for those that seem appropriate for your business and industry.

"People are looking for someone in whom they can place their confidence and trust, and nothing makes a business owner or professional look quite as trustworthy or attractive to potential clients as one who has won awards and recognition," explains Patty Briguglio, MMI Associates.

For example, in these days when accounting irregularities can bring down entire companies and ruin employee retirements, an upstanding and ethical accountant like Cindy Anderson draws clients who want to feel they are in safe hands. Cindy is managing partner of CD Anderson, P.A., a full-service CPA firm that sets itself apart from others by establishing personal relationships with each of its clients. As a trusted business advisor first and an accountant second, Cindy exercises sensitive professional and moral judgments with her clients, always upholding the highest standards. Cindy recently was awarded recognition in the 2006 Class of *Business Leader* magazine Women Extraordinaire.

"Cindy has been a client of ours since 2004, and this is the most recent of a string of awards she has won since then," explains Patty Briguglio. "As a result of these awards, Cindy has seen steady increases in the number of referrals from her existing clients, plus a growing stream of new clients. Cindy's awards are testimonials to her excellent standards and professionalism, and her clients appreciate that fact."

Recognition for your company also helps improve employee morale. Neutral Posture marketing manager Cortney Tenhet says, "It is a great pat on the back for us to receive awards. Our employees are always thrilled when our CEO, Rebecca Boenigk, receives awards, because she thanks everyone for the part they play in her success."

Additionally, awards have given Neutral Posture credibility in their industry. The company won the Attendees Choice Award from the National Ergonomics Conference and Exposition, which is based on peer voting. It was also named the UPS Supplier of the Year for 2003. And winning the Ernst & Young Entrepreneur of the Year Award in Manufacturing resulted in the company attracting potential financiers. "In Rebecca's acceptance remarks, she mentioned what an honor it was to be recognized as a woman-owned business, especially since, not many years before, she and her mother, who was also her business partner, could barely get financing without their husbands' signatures. When she was finished accepting the award, there was a line of bankers with their business cards out ready to greet her as she left the stage," Tenhet notes.

A couple of cautionary notes about awards, however: Don't get so carried away in winning awards that you take your eye off the ball of building your company . . . and don't believe your own PR. Many businesses have crumbled because the CEO bought into her own hype.

Allison Evanow of Square One Organic Vodka subscribes to this philosophy for her up-and-coming company:

> We set realistic expectations and make sure we don't believe our own hype. We make sure we cross all our t's and dot all the i's. The idea has proven to be a good one judging by our early success; but the final success will be determined by how well we can actually run the company beyond just having a great idea. So when people say to us, "Oh, you are going to be huge. This is going to be so successful," I always thank them and then tell myself, "This is great validation that you are on the right path, but you still have to actually do it, and make it happen."

Nothing can take a business down faster than a CEO with a big, out-of-control ego. When you are running a successful business operation, everybody thinks you've got a kabillion dollars anyway. Throw a big ego on top of that, and you have the ingredients for a disaster.

I won't share any names with you, but I have watched a number of women business owners ruin their businesses because they were blinded by the spotlight. One woman does about $10 to 12 million in revenue annually, yet for as long as I have known her, her business has been operating on the edge. If you met her, however, you'd be impressed by her list of awards and recognitions. You'd assume her company is rock solid. But her insatiable desire for recognition leaves her little time to focus on the health of her company. As a result, her business doesn't have a great reputation in terms of credit and integrity. But—hey—she's got all those awards, and she's had her picture taken with lots of famous people.

Enjoy the Rewards of Networking

Networking is one of my favorite things, and I am a firm believer in the value of it. That's why I don't understand why women often say they don't have time to network. How can you not have time to network?

A strong network is one of the most valuable assets you can have for your business success. A strong network can assist you in opening doors to new business opportunities, find dynamite employees, identify professional resources, and provide advice and assistance. I regularly receive e-mails from people in my network looking for a resource or requesting assistance in finding a new employee. We know from research that women owners of million-dollar firms are well-networked. The Center for Women's Business Research shows that these women are more likely to be members of professional groups or associations than other women business owners.

My network of amazing women is vast. I know inspiring, successful women in almost every city in the country today. Therefore, I wasn't surprised when I was asked to recommend speakers for a Web seminar series that the names of these women immediately came to mind while I struggled to think of men who would be good participants. Not that the men aren't out there, it's just that the amazing women I know are on the top of my list.

Susan Phillips Bari, president emeritus and founding architect of WBENC and now president of FlyFast, LLC, says she is fanatical about networking and stresses the importance of it. "My husband, Dick, jokes that whenever I enter a room I start a receiving line. Networking exposes you to a whole new world of possibilities."

"One of my employees created a saying for me: 'I may not look like I am working, but I am really networking.' I keep a very up-to-date contact database because, in business, it's not just whom you know but whom those people know, and so on. Resources and referrals are what make the business world rotate, and my database and networking opportunities are the axis on which everything turns. I share this philosophy all the time, because it is so easy to use and because it always works," says Ellen Fisher, the founder of Greater Philadelphia Women's Yellow Pages.

Kleenslate founder Julia Rhodes found it wasn't easy to go into a world of business that was dominated by men. She learned it was important to have a network. She says:

> You have to join organizations and participate and stay involved. You know, you show up, you show up, you show up. Seventy-five percent of business is showing up and developing those relationships and following through.

Erin Fuller is the executive director of NAWBO, the National Association of Women Business Owners. She says, "The greatest benefit NAWBO members cite in each biannual survey we conduct is being able to network with other women entrepreneurs at the local level. Over two-thirds of NAWBO members do business with other NAWBO members. So clearly, joining a networking organization can make an significant impact on your bottom line." According to Fuller:

> We believe there is something special and unique about connecting with other women CEOs who face the same challenges in terms of personnel and vendor management, business

development opportunities, access to capital, and key markets. And we strongly encourage any entrepreneur, at any level, to reach out to others with shared experiences.

Keep in mind, the best and easiest way to acquire new customers is by word of mouth. Networking can help you create an army of unpaid marketers for your firm.

"Ninety-five percent of my business comes from networking with the corporate members of the National Minority Supplier Development Council and WBENC. I have served in several positions with these groups, and that's where my business comes from," explains Avis Yates Rivers, CEO of Technology Concepts Group, Inc.

Building a network can also be a great resource for your business. "There are lots of people out there who really do want to help you if you just ask. It is amazing. If you get into a situation and say, 'Gosh, I am looking for some feedback,' everybody wants to give you some feedback. Then you have to sort through it all, and a lot of times there is good information out there just for the asking," notes Barbara Woyak of Future Trends Technology Management.

So the next time you say to yourself, "I don't have time to network," think again and make time.

Go for the Gold

It takes just as much work and effort to land a small client as it does to score a big one—so why not go for the gold? A lot of the research on women-owned firms with million-dollar plus revenues demonstrates they serve larger clients. That makes sense, doesn't it? But it's difficult for women-owned firms to access these markets. According to the Center for Women's Business Research, women-owned businesses in the United States are getting an average of 4 percent of corporate dollars spent on outside goods and services. That's certainly not a fair slice of the pie.

"What still needs to be accomplished for women business owners is opportunities. We still struggle with getting into large businesses. So what can we do to rally the troops, to start networking better to help women through supplier diversity channels to help us sell our business and give us the same opportunities given to companies owned by men. What can we do to have an even playing field?" asks Brenda Loube.

For more than nineteen years, Loube and her business partner, Sheila Drohan, have owned Corporate Fitness Works, which customizes fitness programs and wellness services for corporations, government agencies, and retirement communities that include fitness facility planning, design and implementation; fitness center management and evaluation; and fitness and wellness consulting. Their conviction is to set the standard for creating well cultures that encourage individual and organizational well-being.

In an effort to level the playing field, Loube, like many women business owners, certified her company through the Women's Business Enterprise National Council (WBENC), which is the largest third-party certifier of women-owned firms in the country. Founded in 1997, WBENC advocates for women-owned businesses as suppliers to America's corporations by working with representatives of corporations to encourage the utilization and expansion of supplier/vendor diversity programs. Its certification is accepted by nearly all the major corporations in the United States.

Roz Lewis, who runs one of the WBENC certifying partner organizations, says:

> There are many challenges for women business owners, including getting bid opportunities. Women-owned businesses are not being taken seriously as a major component of the supply chain for major organizations. But many corporations are beginning to understand the value that women-owned businesses bring to their bottom line. It gets back to supply chain

management. If you invest in me, then I am able to invest in you, and that is the key. If corporations are not investing in these women-owned businesses, they in turn are not going to be able to turn around and support the corporation's product or service.

"Certification has been very advantageous for us. Many clients we work with require certification. It has helped us open doors that weren't open to us before," says Regina Mellinger, CEO of Primary Services, a Houston-based staffing company, which grosses more than $30 million annually.

In addition to certification for women-owned firms, there is also certification for minority-owned businesses through the National Minority Supplier Development Council. The NMSDC's primary objective is to provide a direct link between corporate America and minority-owned businesses in an effort to provide increased procurement and business opportunities for minority businesses of all sizes.

Avis Yates Rivers has been involved with the NMSDC for fifteen years. "It provides access to most major corporations and tens of thousands of small businesses across the country. So if I am looking to reach out to a firm in Oregon or California, I have a network I can utilize to find what I need. It has fostered relationships across the country that money couldn't buy for me. If I ever need to talk to someone at the big corporations, I know someone there, and I know I can get in the door," explains Yates.

Bag the Big Business Deals

While certification is an excellent marketing tool, Cara Shelton-Kass, chief operating officer of Hi-Tech Imaging, says you have to remember to ask for the business. "I think the most important thing for Women Business Enterprises (WBEs) to remember is to ask for business. I spent three years volunteering at a WBENC partner council, meeting people, and I never asked them for business. I wondered, 'Why are they not giving me opportunities?' One day I asked, 'How come you've never invited me into your company and let me pitch procurement?' And they said, 'You've never asked.'"

"Women are too often concerned about how they're perceived," says Susan Bari. "They don't want to appear to be boastful or forceful, but sometimes they have to be that way. They have to market their businesses and get their names out front. Certification as a WBE is only the first stage in marketing strategy. They really have to be determined, patient and persuasive. They have to believe in what they're doing and show that self-confidence to buyers.[2]

Women often hesitate to ask for the sale. They are good at developing relationships, but they hesitate pushing for the business. Rarely does business drop in your lap. If it were that simple, everyone would own a million-dollar business. You have to make opportunities happen, and believe it or not, no matter what type of business you are in, there is a big customer out there for you.

Margaret McEntyre is the founder of Candy Bouquet, International, one of the fastest growing franchises in the United States and the largest candy franchise in the world. "I have franchisees who work with major corporations and supply candy bouquets for service anniversaries, birthdays, and special events," she explains.

In order to bag the big business deals, you should have a focused strategy. Start by making a list of companies with which you'd like to work. Then do your research. Learn as much about them as you possibly can.

Jill Konrath is the author of *Selling to Big Companies* and founder of the popular Web resource, SellingtoBigCompanies.com, which is a women-owned business. She says:

> To be more attractive to big companies, women-owned firms first need to understand what's going on in these larger organizations. Corporate decision makers today are under tremendous stress. They're expected to attain ever-increasing objectives

with fewer resources and less time. Their calendar is booked solid. They get 150 e-mails each day and twenty to thirty phone calls from sellers who want to meet with them. Time is their scarcest commodity. As best they can, they protect themselves from interruptions. They seldom answer the phone, roll all calls to voice-mail, and rarely call anyone back.

Think creatively when you build your list. Everyone is going to be after the obvious companies. Try to identify other firms that might also be interested in your offerings.

Konrath advises to target no more than ten companies. "You'll be much more successful if you invest time really getting to know these accounts versus trying to get into every big company you possibly can. Most people are scared of pursuing fewer accounts, but this truly is the route to success.

She also believes in thinking small to get a big opportunity by breaking big companies down into bite-sized chunks. "Don't try to get into GE. Instead, focus on getting your foot in the door of a functional unit (sales, engineering, legal, HR) of a division of a business unit," she explains.

You also want to look big. This goes back to the branding we discussed in the beginning of this chapter. Large companies need to have confidence in your ability to get the job done. If you look like you might go out of business next week, you're not going to bag the big one. You want to appear as professional as possible. Make sure you have a professional website, not one that looks like it was created by your niece in high school. Ask yourself whether your company is one with which you'd want to do business.

Whenever possible turn cold calls into warm calls. Through your network of business contacts, ask for leads within the company you are targeting. Even though they may not be the right contacts for your particular product or service, they may be able to make the necessary introductions and get you in the door.

Speak their language. Every large company has its own culture and terminology. Understanding the language your big prospect speaks. Using that language in correspondence and presentations will give you an edge. You'll seem like a good fit for their organization.

Be creative. Don't offer cookie-cutter solutions. Anyone can do that. Bring something new and valuable to the party. Big companies need small business partners, because small firms are more flexible and innovative. Frequently, a big company will look for a small business to partner with to get things done more quickly and efficiently. Therefore, your job is to look at the opportunity, listen to what they need, and then learn how to provide it to them. That's right, *learn* how to provide it. Many times a large prospect will tell you exactly what they want and how you need to deliver it. So turn off your standard sales presentation and jump in and close the deal.

No stranger to the corporate world, Melanie Sabelhaus went right to the big leagues when she started looking for clients for her corporate housing firm, Exclusive Interim Properties. Thirteen years later she did an IPO and went public on the NASDQ as Bridgestreet Accommodations. She went to London to grow Bridgestreet internationally and called on the same corporate clients she had in the United States. Companies like Price Waterhouse and IBM told her the current providers were all mediocre. They desperately wanted a customer-focused company to work with.

"What they were looking for was customer service," she remembers. Melanie took that information to heart and used it to her advantage to run her company. She designed a system catering to the service needs of these firms and started landing big clients right away.

In addition to providing innovative solutions, Jill Konrath advises bringing big companies information they can use to help them run their business better. Share articles, white papers, and booklets that are educational in nature. Doing this demonstrates your commitment to making a difference, versus just making a sale.

"Communicate with them like a peer. Just because you're selling to them does not make you 'less than.' They respect people who share insights, challenge their opinions, and provoke thinking," she adds.

Don't Put All Your Eggs into One Basket

When you rely on one customer or one vendor for the majority of your revenue, you are only one step away from being out of business. Trust me on this one. I learned the hard way.

In the late 1980s, I owned a small, boutique advertising and public relations agency, "small" meaning it was pretty much just me. The business started off doing relatively well. At least I kept my head above water. Then I landed a big client—a deli chain that was franchising across the country. We were all excited as we began developing marketing campaigns, creating graphic standards, and placing media. There were festive grand openings with local celebrities as new franchises start popping up. Everything seemed to be going well.

As they say, appearances can be deceiving. Little did I know that the owners—a married couple—were having marital problem. Things turned ugly when they announced they were getting a divorce. Equal partners in the business, they stymied the growth of the business because they couldn't agree on anything. My unpaid invoices started piling up. Eventually, the business was on the verge of bankruptcy so the couple locked the doors of their headquarters and disappeared. This company represented more than 80 percent of my business. Plus, I owed money to other suppliers that had worked on the account. The writing was on the wall, I had to take down my shingle and return to the corporate world.

A similar situation could have easily destroyed Rebecca Boegnik's company, Neutral Posture, when one of their biggest customers went out of business. "They left us with over $236,000 in uncollectible receivables. We also had a full-time employee dedicated to their account," she says. "Since that time, we have grown our business so that no single customer accounts for more than 5 percent of our sales. I know it is hard to try and control growth, and for most entrepreneurs it is impossible to refuse business. We have just been smart about expanding into other channels of distribution with a varied product line."

Never let your business expansion hinge on the business or the health of one particular company. Diversify so your success won't be destroyed by someone else's failure.

FUND YOUR
BUSINESS GROWTH

FINANCIAL RISK is a reality of being in business. Women who own the larger, faster-growing businesses are willing to take substantial or above-average financial risks to ensure the success of their businesses, according to research from the Center for Women's Business Research.

The more than 400 women business owners surveyed were asked to determine whether they would take substantial or above average risks in regard to their business. More than one out of five (21 percent) said they were willing to take substantial financial risks in expectation of substantial returns when saving or investing for their business, while almost half (45 percent) were willing to take above-average financial risks expecting above-average returns.

Risk taking was consistent among all types of women-owned businesses in the study, regardless of company size, age of business, or personal characteristics of the business owner (age, education, ethnicity, and so on). However, risk taking among women business owners looking to expand their businesses was significantly higher than among women business owners not looking to expand. A willingness to absorb risk is particularly true of women business owners who seek external capital to expand their business, and of those who had successfully sought this type of funding in the past. Twenty-five percent of expansion-oriented business owners are willing to take substantial financial risks, and an additional 51 percent are willing to take above average risks.

"When I started my business, I took a significant risk by venturing into an unfamiliar and somewhat unknown industry," said Judi Henderson-Townsend, founder and president of Mannequin Madness, a mannequin recycler in Northern California. "Four years later, I am looking to expand my business, and I am confident about this next step, as I believe in this business and am willing to take smart risks to ensure its future success."

In addition to being comfortable with financial risk, women-owned businesses that reach the million-dollar threshold also apply sophisticated management practices on a regular basis, especially the use of financial reports to manage cash flow and expenses. If you aren't educated in certain aspects of management—get the education you need. A willingness to learn must accompany your willingness to grow.

There's a funny story about the woman business owner who is meeting with her accountant. He says to her, "I have been preparing your financial statements and I need to point out to you that you are losing money on each of the items you sell. You should revisit your pricing structure."

She replies, "Oh, it's not a problem. I plan to make it up in volume."

This may seem like a ridiculous scenario, but unfortunately there is some truth to it. A failure to really understand your financials can mean the death of your business.

Financial statements tell a story about your company. They provide you with the information you need to evaluate expansion opportunities. They assist you in managing operational expenditures, and they help ensure you are pricing and managing projects appropriately.

As you grow your business, it's easy to undervalue your product or service because you are anxious to get the business. Pricing at fair market value is critical if you want to look credible. Don't be fooled by assuming the business will always go to the lowest bidder. In fact, if you establish your firm as a quality, value-added provider, you shouldn't have to sell based on price alone.

In the early days of my business, one of my dear friends said to me once, "Susan, I am only going to say this one time, and you will never hear it from me again. You don't charge enough." At the time, I was actually bidding on a proposal for her business—can you believe that? So I revised the proposal and learned a valuable lesson.

Think about it this way: If you are pricing your wares significantly lower than your competitors, you look as though you are the "cheap" alternative. Plus, you can risk the financial health of your company.

Utilize your financial statements to determine your most profitable products and services. Review your financials on a regular basis and use them as a guide to adjust your course.

Dawn Stokes of Texas Driving Experience says, "I am so busy with seemingly 'more important' activities that I would glance at financials and know that we were in good shape, but I had not stopped long enough to create a more long-term strategy. Now, I understand this is an important activity."

Finally, if you are seeking financing for your business growth, an in-depth knowledge of your financial statements is critical. Potential financiers expect you to be able to provide an overview of your company's financials and defend your growth assumptions. This isn't something you can hand off to your bookkeeper or accountant. As the CEO, you are expected to be fully aware of the financial health of your firm.

Obtain the Funding

Every business needs money to grow. Depending on your industry and growth plans, the amount you need will vary. As former Congressman Jack Kemp said, "Capital is the seed corn for growth."

But the question becomes, where are you going to get the money you need? The answer is: It depends. I guess you could try buying a lottery ticket and hope you win. However, I wouldn't hold my breath. Funding for business growth comes from a variety of sources. Which ones you select depends on your level of comfort, and many women are not comfortable with finding funding.

Most women-owned firms start off funding their businesses with personal assets, credit card debt, or loans from friends and family. Bonny Filandrinos, for instance, sold her car for start-up cash, and Patty Phillips spent the money she had been saving to buy two polo horses. Linda Drake leveraged her family's personal assets, including her kids' college funds. Typically, start-up capital is about $5,000 to $10,000.

According to research from the Center for Women's Business Research, women business owners' use of capital—both credit and equity—lags behind men. Women business owners are more likely than men business owners to use personal funds or business income to fuel growth. Nearly 60 percent of NAWBO members (National Association of Women Business Owners) list business earnings as a preferred source of capital. Using personal funds or business earnings for growth is okay as long as you choose those methods based on an overview of your available options. But selecting that route because of an unfamiliarity of financing options isn't good. You owe it to yourself, your business and your employees to explore what is available.

"It sounds almost too simple to be true," admits Sharon Hadary, executive director of the Center for Women's Business Research. "But I think women need to be educated in the various types of financial tools and instruments that are available to them."

The Center's research shows that for those women-led companies who did not seek bank loans or lines of credit as a source of capital, the top reasons given were: preferring not to carry debt; not having adequate cash flow to support repayment; believing their company did not quality for this type of financing; and not wanting to risk family or personal assets or financial status.

To accelerate your business growth and to reach $1 million or more in revenues—you'll need fuel to rev up the engine. The Center's research shows larger, faster-growing women-owned firms are more likely to use credit than other firms owned by women. For example, the women-owned firms with revenues of over $1 million are more likely to access commercial loans or lines of credit than are other women-owned firms. But even these larger businesses owned by women lag behind their male counterparts in using commercial credit (56 percent versus 71 percent).

Many women business owners don't feel comfortable in the world of finance, and so they shy away from dealing with outside capital. Successful women are comfortable using OPM (other people's money) to build their businesses.

"Empire builders understand that it is actually less risky to use outside capital in order to grow a business because it means that they are not putting their own capital 100 percent at risk," says Julie Garella.[1]

Lighting manufacturer, Peggy Traub, says, "I never have any second thoughts about money, or asking to borrow money, or making money, or having a big financial goal as a successful entrepreneur. I honestly am happy to say that I managed to avoid those kinds of issues that typically challenge women entrepreneurs."

A desire to grow their businesses, rather than industry, size, or age of the business is the determining factor in women business owners' decisions to seek capital or credit. The Center's research study shows 42 percent of women business owners who obtained business lines of credit and 43 percent who obtained business bank loans wanted their businesses to be as large as possible. This is compared to 29 percent and 32 percent, respectively, of women who had not obtained either of these sources of capital. The study also shows women business owners are not taking advantage of the full range of credit products that are available. For example, 74 percent never considered selling or pledging accounts receivable, 55 percent never considered unsecured personal loans, and 42 percent never considered vendor credit as sources of capital.

According to the research, the women owners of $1-million-plus firms use sophisticated financial strategies. They are different from the women who own smaller firms in that they use a greater number of funding sources, and they use a greater array of financial products.

It's been confirmed by the Center for Women's Business Research that million-dollar-plus businesses take advantage of multiple funding sources, including vendor credit, credit card loans, venture capital and angel investing, bank loans, and other financial strategies.

Begin the Money Hunt

In the most simplistic of terms, there are two types of financing—debt and equity. Debt is when someone loans money to you. Equity is when someone invests in you. Both types of financing have their advantages and disadvantages, but the process to secure either is similar.

Before you start the hunt for money, you should educate yourself about the process. A lack of knowledge can result in a lot of wasted time and a great deal of frustration.

First, make sure you have your business plan and financials in order. (Here we go again. That business plan just keeps popping up.) When you are looking for money, your business plan is like your sales pitch. One of the first things you'll be asked for is a copy of your Executive Summary. Don't rely on someone else to develop your business plan for you. Certainly, you can utilize outside experts, but this business is your baby, and you need to know everything that makes it tick. You must be well-equipped to answer any questions and defend your business assumptions.

Potential funders will want to know as much about you and your business as possible. If your business is new, be prepared to disclose your personal financial statements. If your business has been around for a while, investors will require several years of company financials. Depending on the situation, your personal financials may also be required even with an established operation.

Of course, the potential investor will need to know how much money you want to raise. A big deal killer is asking a banker, "How much can I borrow?" Be prepared to state exactly what you need and how you are going to use those funds. These should be precise. Many financial experts note that women often fall short here. They fail to ask for the amount they really need, and as a result they don't get the adequate capital to ensure their success. Undercapitalization is one of the top reasons for business failure. If you need $4 million, ask for that amount. Don't lowball the number and think you can get by. Your business model should demonstrate how, with the investment, you can grow the company and what the profitability will be.

In addition to learning about your business, funders want to know a lot about who you are, as well as any other key management team members. What is your background and experience? Why are you the right person to build this business? Generally speaking, it's difficult to get someone to invest in you unless you have a solid track record of experience.

When you are applying for a business loan, keep in mind banks are in the business of loaning money. That's their product and that's how they make money. So don't hesitate to shop around and make sure you select a bank that understands your business and has experience dealing with small businesses. Make an appointment and meet with the lender prior to submitting your application.

A number of financial institutions now have specific programs designed to reach out to women business owners, and some have created significant lending initiatives. Wells Fargo was one of the first.

"Wells Fargo recognized early on that women-owned businesses were an under-served market and we established programs to provide financial products and services to facilitate their growth," said Joy Ott, regional president for Wells Fargo Bank in Montana and Wells Fargo's Women's Business Services national spokesperson.[2]

If you get turned down, don't give up. Don't let your dreams die in a bank parking lot. Sometimes you must hear a lot of no's to get to a yes. Or, as Laurie Lumenti Garty, Relationship Manager in SVB Silicon Valley Bank's Emerging Technologies practice says, "You have to kiss a lot of frogs."

Whatever type of financing you are seeking, in most cases it's not going to be fast or easy. The best advice I can give is this: Be patient, Be prepared, and Be persistent.

Even with three large contracts in their hands, Brenda Loube and her business partner, Sheila Drohan, were turned down for a bank loan to get their company off the ground. "Believe it or not, Sheila's mom, a widow at the time, took out her first mortgage on her house for us to use to get started with Corporate Fitness Works," Loube says.

The Center's research shows successful women business owners are persistent in their pursuit of credit or equity. When turned down by one source while seeking business lines of credit, over half (58 percent) approached a different lender or lenders.

Ask for feedback from the lender or investor and learn from the experience. The next time, you may be able to adjust certain aspects of your presentation to get a favorable response. Women who have been successful with funding activities often find they must make changes in their business reports—producing more financial statements or creating or modifying their business plans—to make their companies more attractive to lenders.

Don't be afraid to ask for referrals. It may be a situation where the lending institution doesn't fund companies in your industry, but it may be able to suggest someone else who does. The same is true for equity investors. If they decide to pass on the deal, many will recommend other firms that might be a better fit for you and your business.

Get Credit When You Don't Need It

A fast-growth company often finds itself with a cash flow problem. At that point, the owner typically tries to get a short-term loan or line of credit to bridge the gap. However, even if you are successful in obtaining the funds, the length of time to process the loan can be problematic. When you need cash, you need cash now.

To avoid a cash crunch, get a line of credit from a bank when you *don't* need it. Funny thing about banks: They don't want to lend you money when you need it, but they are eager to loan it to you when you don't.

The other benefit of obtaining a line of credit is it allows you to establish a relationship with a bank and demonstrate you are a good credit risk. That's important when you are trying to get your company funded. As Laurie Lumenti Garty explains:

> Generally speaking, entrepreneurs want to begin laying the groundwork for their company to establish its own credit from day one by maintaining payment terms as agreed upon with their vendors and banks, and by establishing good trade references. Once a company is able to demonstrate it can establish its own credit, a business owner will be able to move away from the strength of the founder or entrepreneur's personal credit and establish credit for the company on its own. At this point, a small business line of credit is something a business owner may want to consider. It can be used for myriad things,

including smoothing out receivable turns, cyclical inventory demands, and business expansion.

According to Garty, the pros of establishing a credit line for a small business early on are twofold. First, it no longer puts a drain on the entrepreneurs' personal credit and enables a company to build its own credit for future needs. Second, it can be a great umbrella to help shield a company in difficult times in the future.

However, she cautions about a down side that should be considered. "Companies must be careful about becoming too leveraged, or about utilizing funds to fuel growth, purchases, or expansions that cannot be supported by the company's revenues or current business environment. Debt always has to be repaid. If a company borrows too early in its life cycle, it may find that the debt payment puts too significant a drain on its cash," she notes.

Get to Know People in the Investment Community

Like most women, Avis Yates Rivers used personal money to fund her business. Then, she secured a small bank loan as a result of being a client of the New Jersey Small Business Development Center. Major funding didn't come until she had the pleasure of sitting next to the CEO of a bank at a luncheon in Washington, D.C. The governor of her state had selected several corporate and small business leaders to meet the newly elected President Bill Clinton.

"We were seated at lunch, and this man asked if it would bother me if he lit a cigarette. I didn't know who he was, but it was such a high to meet the president that even though I am a reformed smoker, I said 'no.' We started talking, and I learned he was a banker. So I told him what I do. Then we got into a conversation about the difficulty of getting access to capital for firms like mine in the service-oriented business. He was just floored. He had no idea this problem existed," says Yates Rivers.

The bank CEO asked her to put together a group of firms that were having difficulty gaining access to capital to meet with him. "I followed through, and we arranged a breakfast in his executive suite in Newark. He went around the table and heard everybody's story. Without hesitating he said, 'I am funding every single one in this room.' Well, his vice president had to be helped up off the floor. He just told the vice president to make it happen. And he did come through on the promise," she explained.

Yates Rivers says her current funding came from knowing another bank CEO. "We sat on the board of the chamber together. I went to see him one day and said I need funding. Because of my relationship with him, the bank funded me."

At this point, you are probably thinking, it can't be that easy. Honestly, it's not. But there is no denying the importance of networking in the investment community. Ask professionals you know, such as your accountant or attorney, if they can make introductions for you. They may have clients or contacts that can also help. Two-thirds of women business owners rely on external accountants or financial specialists for advice about financing their businesses. As Laurie Lumenti Garty says:

> An entrepreneur's network of business associates can be as important as a brilliant business idea and a solid business plan when it comes to getting a startup off the ground. Similar to the four Cs used in evaluating diamonds, lenders use five Cs to evaluate credit risk: character, capacity, capital, collateral, and conditions. Since character takes time to establish, it is wise for business owners to make the time to get to know people in the finance community and establish solid relationships with firms that will be able to help them in the long term.

Talk with other business owners who have successfully acquired capital for their business. Many times they will be happy to introduce you to their source, because they've already been down the road you are traveling and appreciate how difficult it can be.

If you are looking for an equity investment, it is equally, if not more, critical to know the investor community. According to a Diana Project Report on the role and participation of women in the venture capital industry, the existence of pre-existing relationships provides an important link between entrepreneurs and venture capitalists. Lacking connections to equity investors means women business owners have less of a chance of getting their companies funded.

When my partners and I were seeking venture capital, we sent our Executive Summary to venture firms around the country. More often than not, we wouldn't even get a response. When we did it was usually, thanks but no thanks. We felt as though we were invisible. Why couldn't they see what a great company we were building? Why wouldn't they talk to us?

One firm posted the answer loud and clear on its website. In so many words it said, "If you don't know someone who knows us—don't bother."

Another entrepreneur, Lois Landau, whose company develops software that personalizes direct-marketing campaigns, paid $3,000 to pitch to an angel investment network. Afterwards, she heard nothing. "It's all about relationships. I didn't have a strong enough relationship with individuals in that group," she says.[3]

Perfect Your Pitch

When you are looking for funding to grow your company, you need to learn how to sell your company just like you sell your product. You need to be able to tell your story and share you vision in a compelling way. You also need to learn to speak the language of the investment community.

Presenting to investors is no different from making any other type of presentation. You need to research your audience and understand what it is they want to hear. Also, keep in mind even though you *could* speak for hours about your business, you only have a short time to make the sale when you pitch. Typically, your presentation should be no more than a maximum of 10 to 15 minutes. Stay on point. Don't ramble aimlessly through anecdotes because you'll get off track and miss your message. Also, if you must use PowerPoint slides, don't let them be a crutch, and don't make them so full of information your audience spends time reading your slides instead of listening to your message.

Amy Millman is the president of Springboard Enterprises, which assists women-led high-growth enterprises in raising investment capital. "We learned a lot by talking to bankers around the country," she says. "They said women come in and give long stories about their mother bringing them up, or whatever, and why they're doing this and that. Great stuff, but it doesn't tell the bankers what they need to hear and it doesn't end up with a loan being made."

In my opinion, programs to help you hone your pitch are critical. I have been presenting in front of audiences nearly my entire life, so you'd think this process would have been a piece of cake for me. To the contrary. Standing in front of an audience, or pitching one-on-one isn't intimidating for me, but what was eye opening was the nature of what needed to be communicated quickly and effectively to the investment community.

I participated in a program sponsored by the Women's Technology Cluster in San Francisco. In order to be accepted into the program, I had to pitch to a panel of venture capitalist judges. Once selected for the boot camp training, I traveled from St. Louis to San Francisco once a week for nearly six weeks to attend full-day seminar sessions. Three coaches were assigned to help me develop and perfect my pitch—all with the goal of presenting to an audience of venture capitalists at the end of the program. When that day arrived, out of twenty-seven women-led technology companies presenting, SBTV.com was selected as the 2006 Best Investment Opportunity. The hard work, education, and training paid off, and the coaching was priceless.

Angel Investors

Angel investors are one type of equity investors. But don't be fooled by the name. They aren't benevolent people doling out cash to needy businesses. They are typically affluent individuals who are willing to invest in high-risk, start-up business ventures in return for equity and a high return on their investment.

Angel capital fills the gap between what's known as family-friendly funding and venture capital. It is becoming more and more prevalent in the United States. According to the Center for Venture Research, there are approximately 225,000 active angel investors in the United States. Researchers found the angel investor market grew 2.7 percent in 2005, for an investment total of over $23 billion dollars. The University of New Hampshire research credits those angel investments for the creation of about 227,000 news jobs in the United States during that period.

Because angel investors are private individuals, it can be difficult for entrepreneurs to find them. But today, more and more are joining angel investment groups. The number of angel groups increased by nearly 60 percent from 2002 to 2005, from an estimated 150 to 250 three years later, according to an analysis by the Angel Capital Education Foundation (ACEF) and the Ewing Marion Kauffman Foundation. The survey of angel group members of the Angel Capital Association also revealed that the average angel group invested $1.45 million, and that the average angel group invested $387,000 per company during calendar 2005.

To attract an angel investor, you must demonstrate good financials and high-growth potential. You must also have a product that is scalable, with a market opportunity of at least $1 billion. You should have some "barriers to entry" in place, such as an intellectual property portfolio and a realistic exit strategy. Angels also want to see passion and will hold you accountable for results.

Because angel investors take an equity stake in your company, they usually take a seat on your Board of Directors. Stephanie

Hanbury-Brown is the founder of Golden Seeds, a company that supports women entrepreneurs by providing capital to early stage women-owned businesses through its Angel Investor Forum. She says that it needs to be clear what decisions the Board will be responsible for, and what decisions will remain with management:

> The need to change your decision-making process therefore does indicate a loss of control in some respects, but another way to look at it is that the entrepreneur now has some experienced and interested advisors to help with the big decisions. Angel investors are extremely pro entrepreneurs. They do not want to take over. They want the entrepreneurs to be successful, and they want to support them in that success. They will help them gain access to clients, business partners, and other sources of capital.

Golden Seeds started making investments in 2005, and the majority of their portfolio companies are doing very well. "Perhaps our best story is Artemis Woman, a company we invested in when their revenues were only $500,000, and just eighteen months later they were over $3.5 million. This is the sort of momentum we hope for all our investments," notes Hanbury-Brown.

Venture Capital

Venture capital is money provided by professional investors who invest in relatively young, rapidly growing companies that have the potential to develop into significant economic contributors. Research from the Center for Women's Business Research shows only 4 percent of the women business owners with revenues of $1 million or more obtained, or intended to seek, equity investment, compared with 11 percent of comparable men-owned firms.

One reason for the low number is that equity financing is less understood than other forms of financing. The Center's research found more than two-thirds of women business owners responding to the survey (68 percent) indicated they lacked sufficient understanding of the process of obtaining equity from investment firms. Equity is more likely to be considered an option among women who want to grow large businesses. More than half (52 percent) are confident their companies could return a profit for investors, and owners of larger companies were even more confident than owners of smaller firms by a margin of 59 percent to 47 percent.

When considering an investment, venture capitalists (VCs) carefully screen the technical and business merits of your company. Typically, VCs are looking to identify those companies that have the potential to generate $100 million in revenues in ten years or less.

Before you consider venture capital funding, you need to make sure it is the type of investment you'll be comfortable with. You need to weigh what's important to you in terms of your company moving forward. If control is a big factor, then a venture capital investment may not be appropriate. According to Julie Garella:

> Growing with the use of outside capital seemed to be a foreign concept to these women business owners. In fact, most of them said they had not thought about using outside capital, wouldn't know how to get it, and in most cases wouldn't know what to do with it. These business owners expressed pride in the fact that they were debt free, even though it was keeping them from reaching the next level of maturity. Nearly every woman with whom we spoke liked owning 100 percent of her company, and that concept of owning a smaller slice of the pie wasn't one with which they were particularly comfortable.[4]

A VC expects to have some control over your business, and many entrepreneurs, particularly women, aren't interested in giving up control. How much control varies with different firms. Typically, depending on the size of their investment, a venture firm will often want to place one or two members on your company's Board of

Directors. They also often seek to protect their investment by actively overseeing the management of your company and requiring that certain fundamental business decisions receive their prior approval. It is not uncommon for them to replace you as the CEO and bring in someone who they believe is more experienced in that role, which can be difficult for some owners. The founder and managing director of Levensohn Venture Partners, Pascal Levensohn, says most venture-backed companies experience at least one chief executive officer change as they evolve from a startup to a fully integrated company.[5]

Research from the Center for Women's Business Research shows overall only 21 percent of women business owners surveyed agree they were willing to give up some control of their business in return for capital. However, those women business owners whose business goals were related to creating jobs, building great wealth, or of fulfilling a personal vision were twice as likely to be ready to give up control for capital, compared to those who did not have these goals.

"Most of our companies in the Springboard program don't have a concern about control; however, once they see the term sheet that may change. You don't want to inflict the venture process on anybody who is not really prepared for it," explains Amy Millman of Springboard.

Nancy Evans, who was one of the original founders of iVillage.com, met with me shortly after we launched SBTV.com. Because she had grown iVillage from her bedroom to a large, successful, ventured-backed entity, her advice meant a lot to me. During our meeting she told me I'd reach a point where I'd face a fork in the road, and I'd have to decide whether I wanted to have a big piece of a little pie, or a smaller piece of a big pie. She also said only I would be able to make that decision for myself.

So the question you must ask yourself is: "Do I want a big piece of a small pie, or a small piece of a really big pie."

If you decide you want to go after the big pie, venture funding can be a smart choice. However, make sure you choose the VC firm wisely. Not all VCs are created equal. Do your homework and select firms that will be a good fit. If VCs decide to invest in your firm, they will actively work with your company and your management team by contributing their experience and business savvy gained from helping other companies. It's not just about taking a check for a lot of money and saying, "See you later." You want to select a VC that can truly add value.

Make a list of VC prospects you think would be a good strategic partner. There are some investors who simply aren't going to be interested in you. Check out their websites and look at the kinds of companies they have funded in the past. Many firms focus their investment efforts on specific industries, stages of development, geographic locations, and investment amount.

Furthermore, while venture funding can help you grow your business more rapidly, the VC wants to see an exit from the investment in three to seven years. So you need to determine what your exit strategy will be. I'll talk more about exit strategies later in the chapter.

Overcome Gender Bias

Before you begin to chase any type of equity capital, you should be aware it's a difficult and often lengthy process. Also understand that for a woman-owned business it's going to be more challenging because of an inherent gender bias in the system.

The VC world is a clubby market, and women have not been successful at breaking through. A study released by VentureOne, a unit of Dow Jones, shows the number of women-owned or women-run businesses backed by venture capitalists has been on a slippery decline since 2002.

Like it or not, women-led companies are being judged more harshly than those led by men. That's why it is imperative to be well educated about the process before you jump in. As a women business owner seeking capital, you aren't going to be given the benefit of the doubt. You have to demonstrate you really know your stuff—that you are a leader and you know what it's going to take to grow your company.

Two professors from the Olin School of Business at Washington University in St. Louis decided to test the hypothesis that women who owned and/or led businesses are judged more critically than their male counterparts. What they found confirmed the issue of gender bias.

Lyda Bigelow, assistant professor of organization and strategy, and Judi McLean Parks, the Reuben C. and Anne Carpenter Taylor Professor of Organizational Behavior, found that regardless of identical qualifications, investors were overwhelmingly inclined to favor firms run by males over female-run firms.

To reach this conclusion, the two professors created a prospectus for a company that was ostensibly positioning itself to go public. The duo distributed the document along with the CEO's bio to people educated in business finance and asked them if they would consider investing in the company. They sent out two versions of the prospectus, with the company description and the qualifications of the CEO almost identical except for the name and gender of the CEO. The reactions were amazingly different.

The response to the female CEO was reflected in more than just fiscal decisions. Overall, the female CEO was evaluated more harshly in a variety of ways. Investors were willing to compensate female leaders with only 86 percent of the amount they would pay their male counterpart. Conclusions were drawn that the women had less leadership experience and would be unable to resolve a deadlock on the board of directors or manage a crisis situation. According to McLean Parks:

> What we found is that the CEO's sex affected just about everything. We asked what percent of their investment money they'd put into the firm, and it was astonishing. Participants were willing to invest 300 percent more in a firm led by a man. By making stereotypical assumptions about the woman's capabilities,

the IPO became less attractive, which means that female-led firms hoping to go public will have a much harder time finding backers, even though research indicates that the chances for success are just as likely—if not more likely—than for a company run by a male.

McLean Parks doesn't believe people deliberately stereotype females. "I think it creeps in when you have an ambiguous situation, especially an investment situation in which there are some risks. But people did reveal biases they might not have known they had. When we compared the biases to see if they were based on reality, we found they weren't," she notes.

While McLean Parks knew gender bias would have some impact on the research results, she was surprised at just how much of an effect it had. "I didn't expect people to be willing to invest three times as much money in a firm run by a male as supposed to a firm run by a female. That surprised me quite a bit," she says.

The fact that there are very few women in leadership positions at venture capital firms has an impact on the process for women. According to a Diana Project Report on the role and participation of women in the venture capital industry in 1995, women represented only 10 percent of management-track venture capitalists, falling slightly to 9 percent in 2000, despite significant growth in the industry. Sixty-four percent of the women in the industry in 1995 were no longer in the industry in 2000, compared to 33 percent for males. Because of this high turnover, few female venture capitalists gain sufficient experience to become partners and to achieve high visibility in the industry.

As a result of this gender bias, women-owned companies are largely overlooked and locked out of lender and investor networks, which remain overwhelming male. McLean Parks says they were able to determine in their research that it was the male participants who really drove the results:

Female participants didn't see a difference between males and females, at least not a statistically significant difference in terms of their willingness to invest. I think over time we'll see the effect lessen, particularly as more and more women are running their own businesses and become visibly successful as CEOs and business owners at top levels of management.

Let me share a couple of real life stories which further confirm this research. First, a few years ago, SBTV.com participated in a venture forum. We were thrilled and a little surprised to be one of fifteen companies selected to present to the audience of VCs. I say "surprised" because we really weren't at the stage of development to attract venture capital, but we didn't recognize that at the time.

Of the presenting companies, I was the only female CEO presenter. The evening before the presentation, the event sponsors hosted a networking cocktail reception. When I arrived, my business partners were talking with one of the event coordinators, and as I walked in the room they pointed me out to the gentleman who said, "Oh great. We were hoping she'd be good-looking." It's probably a good thing that I wasn't there to hear that comment, but it made me wonder, "Was I only a token novelty?"

Artemis Woman founder, Lisa Kable, and her business partner also witnessed bias first hand. Kable says, "Ah yes, men and money! Pretty much at every financial presentation we made, usually to a room full of men, the feedback would include something like, 'Can I have a few products and see what my wife thinks about it?' They said they didn't understand these women products. Please, like they understood the nanotechnology presentation right before us? Did they have to ask their wife what they thought about new gene markers in fighting cancer?"

The story gets even better. "At a big business plan competition with hundreds of money people in the audience, the (male) VC/panelist laughed at our products and asked if he could wax his car with our scrubs. They didn't take us seriously. But guess who's laughing now," Kable adds.

Despite the challenges, companies such as Kable's and mine do get equity funding. It isn't impossible if you educate yourself, prepare and go in with your eyes wide open.

Develop an Exit Strategy

Regardless of how you fund your company's growth, you should start thinking about an exit strategy from day one. It only makes sense. Why build a successful million-dollar-plus company only to see it die when you are ready to retire? Your business is your baby. You want to watch it grow up and be able to thrive on its own. In many respects it's your legacy.

To begin developing your exit strategy, make a list of the various options available to you. For example, do you want your employees to be able to purchase the company? There are Employee Stock Option Programs (ESOPs) that are designed to assist employees in purchasing the business over time. Are there competitors who might be interested in acquiring your company? Do you have children you want to groom to take over the business?

Lorri Keenum, CEO of Midwest Trenching and Excavation, a $10 million-plus company, says the issue of an exit strategy played into the selection of her company's name. "A lot companies will include their initials, or a last name on the business. I never felt like that was a real good marketing idea, because when you go to sell it, it's not as marketable. So I started with really a generic name," she explains.

Consult with professional advisors about what exit vehicles might be best for your company, and do that sooner rather than later. Don't wait until your back is against the wall. That's what happened in my own family.

My mother and father owned a very successful funeral home—one of the largest in their area. My mom ran the business operations and dad was the marketing guy. They were an excellent team. Throughout the years, they had discussed the possibility of selling so they could enjoy their "golden years." They had even gone so far as to list or contract with a broker in their industry, but none of the potential buyers passed the personality test for my parents. That's right. They wanted to make sure the person who purchased the business was the "right" kind of person. The broker later told me he believed they never really wanted to sell.

Sadly my mother was diagnosed with Alzheimer's and eventually her care required my father's full attention. So we hired a thirty-nine-year-old young man as the general manager who had grown up in the community, and everything seemed to be okay. And it was until he was diagnosed with cancer and given only a few months to live. We needed to sell the business quickly. The funeral home industry is a tight knit community, and the word quickly spread about the situation my parents were in. The company sold within a few months, but for a much lower price than we would have been able to get had the circumstances been different.

I'm glad my mother didn't understand the terms of the sale, because it would have broken her heart. All those years of working 24/7 wound up being worth a relatively small amount. Don't let this happen to you and your business.

Get acquainted with investment bankers, accountants, and other professionals who support your industry. They can be sources of information about people who are looking to get into the business.

Julie Aigner-Clark was the founder of Baby Einstein, the popular videos that entertain children in a positive fashion. After growing the company to a certain level, she sold to Disney.

"My husband was a physics major, and I was an English major. We never thought we'd be rich. We began to think about how much could we sell this company for. We came up with a number and approached Disney because we were already doing books with them," she says.

Julie says selling to Disney was the greatest moment for her in business. She takes great pride in looking at what Disney has done to the company. "There was some difficulty after selling to Disney. I'm thrilled that we sold and I have no regrets, but I'm sorry I wasn't allowed to continue to be involved. Baby Einstein was my baby. They bought it and said, 'This is Disney now.' That was tough."[6]

Since the first Springboard Venture Forum in 2001, 33 percent of women entrepreneurs have left the companies they founded. Recent research from the Center for Women's Business Research shows that women-owned businesses grossing over $1 million in revenue are just as likely as their male counterparts to have a long-term strategy for selling, handing down, or closing their businesses. In fact, women business owners are nearly twice as inclined as men business owners to intend to pass the business on to a daughter or daughters (37 percent versus 19 percent).

After taking over her father's company, Kathleen Thurmond of Best Washington went back to school for an MBA. One of the first things she learned was the importance of developing an exit strategy. Although she wasn't ready to sell the company, her fellow students started planting the seed with her, and she decided to at least keep an open mind.

"Two companies started calling me in the fall of 2004. They were the big guys in the industry. So I agreed to meet with them, but I told them I really wasn't interested. Then I started getting letters stating how much they were willing to pay, and it's the most they'd ever paid. I ended up really thinking about change," she says.

Kathleen asked herself the question, "Is this really what I want to do with the rest of my life?" Her answer was No. "I ended up negotiating the deal myself. It was kind of neck-and-neck between two big companies until the end. I actually took a little lower price from one company because they would hire my employees. The way it turned out, it was a really great sale. They told me it was one of the best-run companies they had seen and that everything went really smoothly."

The Center's research also shows women business owners are more concerned than men business owners about the buyer's identity, personality, and background; about the buyer's plans for the business; and about plans for current employees. "Given that women are more likely to create a business than to take over an existing one, they likely have a greater sense of responsibility about their people's future and the company's continued success," said Susan W. Sweetser, second vice president, Specialized Markets, MassMutual.[7]

Amy Millman, Springboard's president, says she thinks a lot of women get hung up on the exit strategy:

> They think that when they are gone the whole thing is history, but that's not true. It is just operating in a different fashion. It's like when your kids leave home and build their own lives. They move, they change their name, they move to a different city, but they aren't gone. There is a piece of you that still remains. And, hopefully, there is a piece of you that has an equity stake. I think this is what we as women miss. It's not black or white; you can still own a piece of the company even if you are not in charge of it on a daily basis. Understanding and accepting that the business cycle is a process is also important. You don't have to stay with a company throughout its lifecycle. The most successful women business owners achieve what they want to achieve at one company, and they move on, they get ready, lead the next venture, and are ready with the next point in their future.

Leave a Legacy

Of course, selling your company isn't the only option for your enterprise. Once you have built a thriving business it can become a legacy to pass on to the next generation. In the past, male entrepreneurs handed their businesses over to their sons, but today that scenario is changing. Men are now handing over the reins to their daughters. So are the women.

Phyllis Hill Slater is handing over the reigns of Hill Slater, Inc., a Long Island engineering and architectural support firm, to her daughter, Gina. The company was started by her father, Philbert D. Hill, PE, and both Phyllis and Gina have worked hard over the years to uphold his vision.

"There were five children in my family," explains Phyllis," so my dad always had five employees. Even when he was consulting, before he started the business, he involved us. We'd be out on construction sites holding the other end of the tape measure."

Having been born in the industry, so to speak, and working side by side with her father for many years, Phyllis realized how important her father's contribution was to the business community. "It was a different time back then," she remembers. "He was the only African American in his engineering class and one of an elite group of professional engineers. In fact, he was the chief electrical engineer on the first nuclear power plant in the country. But he always wanted to be the captain of his own ship. He worked so hard and broke so many barriers, that this has been my way of honoring his legacy. And now my daughter, Gina, will keep that vision alive. I feel very strongly that as business owners we walk on the backs of those before us, and it's very important to acknowledge the inroads and sacrifices they made for us."

Patrice Kouvas took over as president of AVI Food Systems, a company her father founded more than forty years ago. "It was exciting, but at the same time it was important to earn the respect and appreciation of all of the people who had worked with him for so many years. And it was hard work to get to a point where they also held that respect," she says.

Currently, AVI operates in seven states surrounding its home state of Ohio, and the company holds three national contracts. Patrice plans on growing into additional states and expanding her national contract base. In addition to growing the company, she has raised two daughters. But she doesn't know if there will be a transition to a third generation. "My daughters have an interest in AVI. They have worked here throughout their teenage years, but they have to understand it has to be something they truly want and are truly committed to. But we are hopeful," she says.

What better way to leave your mark on the world than to create an entity that is bigger than you? Your million-dollar business can continue providing employment and opportunities for years to come.

PART THREE

Accelerating Your
Business Growth

ACCELERATING YOUR business growth means selecting a strategy that best fits your business and your goals. There's no right or wrong path to follow as long as you commit to taking the necessary steps to make it happen and remain true to the core values of your company.

8

DEVELOP GROWTH
STRATEGIES

GROWTH IS BOTH exciting and scary. There are many nights when I can't sleep and I pace the floor worrying about the business. Then there are days when I am bursting with pride as the little company we started takes a giant step forward. It's a crazy roller-coaster ride sometimes—there's no better way to describe it. Just hold on tight and enjoy.

Control the Growth

There is nothing in the rule book that says you have to sprint to the finish line. In fact, growing a business is more like a marathon than a sprint. Unless you are determined to be at $100 million in five years, controlled growth is often a smart move.

Overextending yourself and your resources by taking on too much too fast may kill your business. Rapid expansion can cause you to lose focus, drain your financial resources, and ultimately break the system. You don't want your company to be a flash in the plan. You want its star to shine brightly for a long time.

Square One Organic Vodka founder Allison Evanow says, "I just don't want to completely burn myself out along the way. So the fear is not about the success itself, but how to manage that success in a healthy manner."

When Bonny Filandrinos' company hit the $5-million mark, she realized she didn't like how her own job had changed. She felt she was spending too much time managing people, which took her away from what she felt her strong point was: working with her clients. She made a deliberate choice to downsize. "I figured out our sweet spot was really $3 million with the size of staff that I could manage."

Filandrinos limited her growth to a more manageable rate. "I knew that meant it would limit the size and scope of my company, but I also knew that would make us able to deliver services that were much better than those of our competitors," she explains.

Turning business away helped Lorri Keenum manage her company's growth. "In the first twelve years, we never turned down an opportunity to bid on anything. I mean, we just always got it done. Failure was just not an option. If we had to work all night and the team had to pull everything together and get it done, we did. But the St. Louis Cardinals were requesting bids for a project, and about two weeks before the drop dead date, I realized we didn't have the manpower to get the bid in. And so we turned down work, which is hard. But my business philosophy is controlled growth. I'm very conservative when it comes to making sure we can handle what we have," she explains.

Fast-growth companies typically take shortcuts and hold things together with band-aids and duct tape. It reminds me of a hamster running on one of those little wheels—they go faster and faster but get nowhere. Once your business operations falter, it's difficult to regain your momentum.

As chairman and CEO of National Van Lines, Maureen Beal is the third generation of her family's moving business. She took over from her father, who took it over from his father. Beal's determination to preserve the company's rich family history has helped her create her own business philosophy:

> My core business philosophy is to grow the business, but not too quickly. I want to make sure that we are able to substantiate the growth. I don't want to get too big too fast and not be able to service our customers like we want to service them. Also, more importantly, I don't want to get so big that we don't remember where we come from.

Be realistic about how much you can truly achieve when you develop your growth plans. Take a look at your resources and don't over-extend. Not only will it be stressful for you, but chances are you'll lose customers in the process. Remember, Rome wasn't built in a day, and there is no such thing as an overnight success.

Build Together Through Strategic Alliances

In today's virtual world, many businesses are growing their firms by creating strategic alliances. Forty-five percent of certified Women Business Enterprises report they have formed a joint venture or strategic alliance to bid on an opportunity with a large corporation.[1]

How do you find companies to align with? You probably already know people in your industry or a related industry you could partner with to go after a major contract opportunity. If not, check with your industry association to see if they have any sort of database you could access for this type of business matchmaking. Some associations have newsletters where businesses can advertise for alliance partners. Current clients can also be a good resource. Ask who they might recommend.

Alliances can be created for specific alliances or for ongoing business operations. Beth Bronfman is a perfect example. She started her New York advertising firm, Leibler Bronfman Lubalin, twenty years ago. Today she has grown her company to $40 million in revenue, but she only has twelve employees on her staff. Bronfman realized from the start she had to run a "lean and mean" business to be most efficient. She also realized she had to have the best of the best people working for her, and the best way to accomplish that was, and always has been, through strategic partnerships.

"I needed the top talent but couldn't always pay them what they would need as salary, so using them when I needed them was the best option," she explains.

For example, rather than working with an in-house lawyer, she created a partnership with the top advertising law firm in the country and uses them only when she needs them. She also has strategic partnerships with PR agencies, media buyers, and television producers. These alliances allow her to fulfill a client's needs, while enabling her to cut down on her overhead, in turn passing on the cost savings to her clients. She often splits the commissions with her partners as compensation.

"Our clients have always been happy with this arrangement, because they are getting exactly what they need without having to pay for things they don't need," she says. But she cautions to make it seamless for the client. "I always lead the project so my clients know they can trust the process, and that I will manage their expectations to the fullest," Bronfman adds.

Develop Smart Partnerships

Partnerships can be the kiss of death for a business, particularly when they aren't well thought out. In fact, for many years I counseled business owners against partnerships because I had seen too many disasters. Partnerships are a lot like a marriage. The wrong pairing can really get ugly. There are lots of sad and unfortunate stories of best friends who have partnered to start a business, and who ended up destroying the business and hating each other. There is one significant difference between a partnership and a marriage: You don't have to love each other to be great business partners.

Smart partnerships can help your business grow much faster and more successfully. A good partnership arrangement brings diverse skills and backgrounds to the business. Partners should share your business vision and values, and they should complement your skill set. The whole becomes greater than the sum of the parts with a well-designed business partnership.

Even though you may think you can tackle everything in your business, no one is good at everything, at least no one I know. So think about what you are really, really good at, and then ask yourself what other skills could enhance your company's ability to grow and expand.

Caroline Nault and her business partner saw an opportunity to create a business representing pre-manufactured trade show exhibits twenty-one years ago. Today, Exhibits South is a thriving enterprise with nineteen employees. As Nault says:

> My partner and I complement each other with our abilities, and I think that has a lot to do with our success. We support each other. I don't know how people start businesses on their own. I don't believe I could run a company myself without a partner like I have.[2]

When the opportunity to purchase SBTV.com presented itself, I thought, how perfect! SBTV.com would incorporate all my skills and experience. To a certain degree, that was true. I had marketing experience, television experience, a legal background, and video production experience. What I didn't have was a background in or understanding of technology, and I had only a limited amount of sales experience. A big part of SBTV.com is technology, and our revenue comes from advertising sales.

One option was to outsource or hire staff to handle the technology and the advertising sales, but how do you afford that when you are just starting off? Instead, I sought people to join me as partners in the business who were experts in the areas where I was lacking. My first call was to a man I had worked with who had tremendous experience running and managing sales teams for major companies, Dan Demko. On the technology side, I reached out to Michael Kelley. I had met Michael through associates in St. Louis, and I knew he had an amazing background in developing technology. Fortunately for me, both Michael and Dan agreed to be partners in the business.

Could I have grown the business by myself? Maybe. But certainly not to the level it has grown today in a relatively short time frame. Our combined skills have allowed us to really develop the business and create a sustainable business model much more quickly and easily. Our second year in business we grew the company by 362 percent and broke even.

Lighting manufacturer, Peggy Traub, also sought out the best person she knew in the industry in terms of sales and product development skills when she decided to start her business. "When I first envisioned Adesso, I realized that I would need a partner who knew the manufacturing and sales side of the business. I knew the retail side, so I approached Lee Schaak, an industry expert, and proposed my new concept. He has so many of the skills that I lack, and neither one of us would have been that successful on our own," she says.

Partnerships bring more than diversity in skill sets. They also provide diversity in perspectives and viewpoints. In our company, Michael is a stickler for process, whereas Dan and I tend to be more creative and intuitive. However, when we disagree we all sit down and discuss the situation, and together we come to the best solution. You know the old adage—two heads are better than one. In our case, three heads are better than one.

"Set parameters with partners. If two partners agree on everything, you don't need both. But you must respect each other's differences," advises Beth Bronfman.

If you decide to grow your business by bringing in partners, make sure you have legally protected yourself. You'll need a buy-sell agreement for your company that clearly explains what will happen if something goes wrong and one or more partners want to go their separate ways. Think of it in terms of a prenuptial agreement. If the marriage breaks up, you have to know from the very beginning how you are going to divide the assets.

Think Globally for Growth

Did you know 95 percent of the world's consumers live outside of the United States? If you are only selling your products domestically, you are only reaching 5 percent of the potential market. That's according to the U.S. Department of Commerce.

The huge potential of the overseas market is attracting more and more small businesses to grow from the garage to the globe. The Commerce Department also reports that 98 percent of the growth in new exports comes from the nation's small businesses.

"Small and medium-size businesses that engage in international trade are 20 percent more productive than non-exporters, have 20 percent job growth, and are 9 percent more likely to stay financially solvent," says Janet Shearn, director of customs and trade compliance for United Parcel Service.[3]

The Women Presidents' Organization conducted a survey of its membership and learned that two-thirds were planning to add international locations. Orthopedic surgeon turned entrepreneur, Taryn Rose, is a WPO member and says she was confident her line of footwear would do well internationally. "I felt our product would be well received in other cultures where women are very progressive and independent, like Great Britain and Korea. I also knew it was important to diversify our risks. If the U.S. market has a downturn, we will have business going on elsewhere that would continue without any slow down."

Women business owners who have taken their business beyond our borders say that finding capital for such expansion can be challenging. Additionally, it's not uncommon to exceed your initial cost projections by 10 to 25 percent. The U.S. Small Business Administration offers an Export Loan Guarantee program to small businesses that want to establish or expand export operations, guaranteeing up to $500,000 of commercial financing. In addition, funding can be obtained from the Overseas Private Investment Corporation, the Private Export Funding Corporation, and the Export-Import Bank of the United States.

If you have the capital you need to expand overseas, make sure you do your research. Size up potential markets carefully. Don't assume whatever works here will work in other cultures. With twenty-six offices and 500 employees around the world, Margery Kraus of APCO calls her strategy "Glocal." No, I didn't misspell the word. Margery says:

> It's about being able to have a global strategy for the client but to be able to execute with people who are very knowledgeable in the marketplace. The first thing we learned was not to make the mistake of taking what you were doing successfully in one country and trying to just replicate it. We take concepts and find ways to translate them—to make them more applicable in the local market. The key to making this work is finding really excellent practitioners in each of the countries where we do business.

Rebecca Herwick is a multimillion-dollar women business owner who expanded her company, Global Products, internationally. "I recommend narrowing your focus by concentrating on no more than two or three best prospect markets. Also, if you can find foreign distributors for your product, you'll be able to simply sell them your products and let them worry about reselling them at a profit in their domestic markets. Distributors are nice because they can offer foreign customers top-notch service. They are easier for you to deal with because they typically buy enough of your product to build up an inventory."

Cultivating international contacts before you expand is also important, according to Laurel Delaney, CEO of GlobeTrade.com. "You should have traveled to at least one foreign country and stayed for several weeks, preferably with a native family. You can't hide behind a great website or e-mail forever. Cultivate friendships and watch, listen, and learn."

Although international markets offer tremendous growth opportunities, they also pose additional business risks. So if you are thinking about growing your business into foreign markets, proceed cautiously. Make sure you consult with professional advisors.

There are risks in doing business overseas that you typically don't encounter while doing business in the United States. Before you enter into a foreign transaction with a new customer you need to do credit checking and establish credentials to make sure you are going to get paid in timely fashion on your investment. One of the most serious considerations for those doing business overseas is to avoid violating the Foreign Corrupt Practices Act. Passed in 1977, the FCPA prohibits American companies from making payments to foreign officials for the purpose of obtaining or keeping business. Sounds simple enough, but you can be easily fooled. Watch for red flags, such as excessive commissions, or requests for payments to an offshore bank account or third party. If anything seems unusual or troubling, investigate the contract further. It's also recommended you obtain a statement that the agent will comply with the FCPA and other applicable laws.

Any violation of the FCPA, even an innocent one, can result in serious penalties. The Department of Justice can impose criminal penalties on the corporation, its officers, and its individual employees that can run into millions of dollars.

There are myriad government resources for answers and advice if you are interested in doing business overseas. For example, the Department of Commerce Commercial Service (www.export.gov) offers information on market research, export finance, trade partners and leads, shipping, and document requirements. You can also call 1-800-USA-TRADE to find out whether your company is export-ready.

The Commerce Department has international trade professionals in 108 offices in forty-seven states, and 150 overseas offices in eighty countries, to help U.S. firms sell internationally. The department also has special initiatives for women- and minority-owned businesses.

Make sure you get the help you need before you expand beyond our borders. Don't limit your opportunities. The world can be your market!

Think Franchising for Fast Growth

Franchising has become a popular strategy for growing a business. Franchising allows you to grow with very little capital investment. There are approximately 320,000 franchises in the United States in seventy-five different industries. According to the International Franchise Association, one out of twelve retail businesses in the United States is a franchised business.

Franchising works well for companies with a unique or unusual concept that has a broad geographic appeal, whose operations can be easily duplicated through training and support, and who have a good track record of profitability.

Karen Powell, partner and cofounder of Decor & You, believes franchising is a wonderful business model because it's a win-win for everyone involved. "It's not something you go into lightly, however. You have a successful business model already and you have to have your systems in place."

Two Men and a Truck founder Mary Ellen Sheets started the moving company on a shoestring. To earn money for school, her two young sons used an old beat-up truck to help people move. However, when more and more calls started coming in, the idea to actually start a real business emerged. Even though she had no prior experience running a business, the company took off and she quit her day job to run it full time. Then in a local competition she won a consultation with Deloitte & Touche, who suggested she franchise the concept. It took a year or two to get the franchising off the ground, but it grew quickly from there. Today, Two Men and a Truck boasts $220 million in sales. The company is the fifth largest moving company in the United States, with over 1,300 trucks on the road and 181 franchise locations in the United States, Canada, the United Kingdom, and Ireland. They have plans to expand to Mexico, Australia, and South Africa.

As the head of franchising at Dunkin Brands, Lynette McKee says their Dunkin Donuts stores are 100 percent franchised. There are no company-owned stores. "We looked at how we could grow quickly. Franchising is realistic from a business plan standpoint, for us to show how we can triple in size from 5,000 units to 15,000 by the year 2020," she notes.

To franchise your business, you need several years of profitability and you should have demonstrated the business can be replicated in more than one location. You also need the ability to provide ongoing training and support to your franchisees.

Sona MedSpa began franchising in 1997. Today it has locations in operation across the nation and is a market leader in the medical spa arena. The company's CEO, Heather Rose, is passionate about the franchise model. She talks about their support of franchisees: "We have the necessary support systems in place. We provide the medical and operational expertise. We have a national medical director and training nurses and an internal medical advisory board. We also provide tremendous depths of marketing resources, both from the branding perspective to drilling down into the tactical aspects of the business at the local level. We also provide day-to-day operational support."

Make sure all your intellectual property is protected and consult with an attorney who specializes in franchise law. Franchise organizations must file complex legal disclosure documents with federal and state agencies so it's important to get the right advice up front. If you don't know a franchise attorney, check with your state bar association. The International Franchise Association also has basic information for potential franchisors at www.franchise.org.

Reap the Benefits of Direct Sales

The practice of selling direct dates back thousands of years. Direct selling is the sale of a consumer product or service, person-to-person, away from a fixed retail location. As a result, it requires less capital to expand your business reach. According to the Direct Selling Association (DSA), annual industry sales in 2006 increased to $29.7 billion dollars and the industry's ten-year growth rate is almost 80 percent. There are almost 14 million Americans who work in this industry, and over 80 percent are women. An economic impact study conducted by Ernst & Young found the industry contributed $72 billion to the U.S. economy in 2004. According to Neil Offen, DSA president and CEO:

> The economic impact study confirms the ongoing growth of direct selling as a shopping option for millions of American consumers. In ever-increasing numbers, Americans are choosing direct selling because they enjoy personal contact with knowledgeable sales representatives. Consumers enjoy service, selection, and social interaction that is hard to match with other shopping experiences. A growing number of companies recognize the benefits associated with direct selling—low overhead, robust cash flow, a highly motivated workforce,

and loyal customers among others—and are diving into the direct selling market.[4]

The industry includes global companies with household names—including Avon, Herbalife, Mary Kay, The Pampered Chef, and Tupperware—as well as hundreds of small- and medium-size businesses. One of the best loved American companies—The Longaberger Company, America's premier maker of handcrafted baskets—grew through direct sales. Handcrafted basket-making holds a special place in the Longaberger family going back generations. The Longaberger family moved to Dresden, Ohio, in 1896, and soon thereafter J.W. Longaberger took a job with the Dresden Basket Factory. As a full-time apprentice he meticulously learned the basketmaking craft and mastered the precise, tight weaving style that would become the Longaberger Company's trademark. J.W.'s love of basket-weaving was passed down through the generations, and in 1973, Dave Longaberger, J.W.'s son, founded The Longaberger Company. Today, the Longaberger Company is headquartered in Newark, Ohio and has some 3,100 employees. The company handmakes high-quality baskets using little machinery or automation, and has expanded its product line to include a variety of home and lifestyle products, such as jewelry, wrought iron, pottery, and other items. In fall 2007, it will launch bath and body products. The company also has a destination business, such as the Longaberger Homested and Longaberger Factory Store in Ohio, near Dresden. More than 310,000 people visited Longaberger in 2006. In a commitment to its direct-selling model, the company awards commission and discounts to its home consultants on sales generated at its destinations.

"It grows out of the vision of my father, Dave Longaberger, and his frustration at attempting to build sales through a more traditional retail venue. He believed the best way to convey the handcrafted tradition and rich history was through direct sales, by building relationships with customers on a one-on-one basis. He began selling the baskets himself through home shows and the rest is history," explains CEO Tami Longaberger, Dave's oldest daughter.

The Longaberger family remains committed to high quality and American craftsmanship inspired by the company's talented basket-makers. The 45,000 independent home consultants who sell Longaberger products directly to consumers through home shows today continue to share the company's rich history across America. Says Tami Longaberger:

> It brings me tremendous joy and satisfaction to know that Longaberger continually gives tens of thousands of women the opportunity to be their own boss every single day. We have others who have taken the Longaberger opportunity and turned it into a way to work from home or on a part-time basis while they maintain a primary focus of being full-time moms. The Longaberger opportunity allows them to be involved as much as they want to be. When I see women succeeding on their own terms, I take pride in knowing that Longaberger has helped them achieve their dreams and goals.

After chatting about how they could make a little extra cash, Bonnie Kelly and Teresa Walsh tried a few business ideas that they said were fun, but which didn't really work out. Then they each took $25 from their grocery fund and pursued their passion for Sterling silver jewelry.

"We started designing our own jewelry creations and hosting what we called A Fun Ladies' Night Out Playing Dress-up with Jewelry," the duo explained.[5]

One party led to another and after hearing time and again from partygoers that they'd like to do what Bonnie and Teresa were doing, the two recognized their small business could become a fun and life-changing business opportunity for other women. In 1997, Silpada Designs officially launched.

During the past ten years, Silpada has experienced phenomenal growth. The company has experienced an average of 100 percent growth every year and exceeded $190 million in retail sales in 2006. In 2007, the firm's more than 19,000 representatives across the company should boost sales in excess of $225 million.

Both Bonnie and Teresa believe that life can be as big as you dream. They say they are inspired by the women who have solely supported their families, the women who have found new friends, and the women who have experienced their self-confidence soar.

So whether you choose direct selling, franchising, partnerships, strategic alliances or controlled growth, remember the important criteria is to choose the strategy that best fits your business goals. Furthermore, these strategies are not the only possibilities. Do your research. Ask questions. Investigate. The right approach will ultimately reveal itself.

THE REST OF
THE STORY

THE DISCUSSION of passion I've purposely saved for the end of this book, even though a lot of business books emphasize passion in the first or second chapter. Passion is a popular buzz word—everyone talks about the importance of passion. It's not that I disagree. You have to be passionate about your business to succeed.

However, I also know when you selected this book you did so because you want to be successful. You are already passionate about what you do and you want to make it bigger and better. You want to build a successful business enterprise and you are committed, determined, focused, and inspired.

You've Gotta Love It

Passion is life's energy. When you are building a successful enterprise, working countless hours, and tackling endless challenges, you absolutely need that passion, that energy to keep you going. If you don't have it, you won't be as successful as you could be, and it may nearly kill you in the process. Someone once said to me, "Love what you do and you'll never work a day in your life." That's so true. Passionate entrepreneurs love what they do.

It amazes me how many times people ask me what type of business they should start. They tell me they really want to go into their own business, but they have no idea what they should do. My answer is: Business ownership isn't for you. At least an entrepreneurial business isn't for you. If you don't know what you truly want to do, then I can't answer that question for you.

Entrepreneurs are the creative, innovative inventors who see opportunities. They are change agents. It's the passion and the vision that drives a successful entrepreneur. It's what makes them a star. The common thread of success among wildly successful women business owners is passion. Follow your passion and create your million dollar business.

Define Success for Yourself

Success—a word that means so many things to so many people. I suspect that ultimately we all have to define it for ourselves, because it may have as many meanings as there are people in the world. It isn't just money. It isn't just numbers. It has to happen inside.

—Debra J. Fields, founder, Mrs. Fields Cookies

In order to define what success means to you, answer the following statement in your own words and in your own way:

I know I am successful when _____

_____

_____.

Every one of us will respond differently, and that's what it's all about. Even though our answers may differ, however, it's important that individually we each give an honest answer—an answer that comes from your heart.

As Yogi Berra used to say, "You've got to be careful if you don't know where you are going because you might not get there." As you journey down the road toward business success, you need an internal road map to guide you. What does success look like for you? What does it feel like?

Answering these questions is more difficult than you think. Your answer may easily be shaped by someone else's idea of what success should be for you. Our families, friends, business associates, and advisors all have an opinion of what you should do. It's easy to accept their expectations as your reality.

"Whether you know it or not, you may very well have sold out," says Dr. Phillip C. McGraw in his book, *Self Matters*. He continues by adding that typically when we sell out, we abandon the things that matter to us because we don't want to disappoint anyone.

Phyllis Godwin, CEO of Granite City Electric Supply Company, took over the company which was founded by her father Nicholas Papani in 1923. She believes success means different things at different stages of your life:

> I've lived a long time and I've seen a lot of things evolve. I feel as if I've had so many sequential lives that I define success in different ways. To me, right now in this stage of my life, success is having options to be able to do what I want, when I want, and to have made enough money to support the causes that are important to me. I am able to live in a beautiful place that I enjoy, and I am surrounded with a wonderful family, and I'm healthy. That's success for me now.

Stay True to Yourself

Following your dreams and building a successful business must be underscored by your commitment to your own personal values. Sometimes that's a difficult process. It may mean standing up to family members or friends. Sometimes it means confronting difficult personal issues. But the bottom line is that if you aren't living authentically then success, fame, money—none of it is important. You can't compromise your personal values on the journey to building a million-dollar business. You'll be miserable if you do.

When I was running the company I owned before SBTV.com, I was awarded a huge contract that immediately catapulted my small business to the next level. However, a couple of months into the deal, I realized it was a huge mistake. The relationship with this client deteriorated dramatically, and I felt as though my staff and I were basically being abused and harassed. The work we were being asked to do was not the work we contracted to do, and in fact, was not the work we wanted to do.

For a while, I did my best to roll with the punches. Then, I could see my self-esteem waning and my health was being impacted. I realized it was time to fire this client. My three core personal business values were being compromised: professionalism, respect, and integrity. Without pointing fingers or placing blame, I respectfully resigned from the contract. A lot of people probably thought I was crazy to walk away from such a lucrative deal, but that didn't matter to me. I stood firmly on my values, and I didn't allow the lure of money to draft me into a situation where I would have eventually lost my self-respect.

When you compromise your values and stay mired in a situation that isn't right for you, you close yourself off from other wonderful opportunities. A week after I resigned from that contract, I learned about the opportunity to purchase SBTV.com. If I hadn't fired that client, I would not have been in a position to even consider such a move.

"Really listen to your customers and fire the customers you can never satisfy," says Tessa Greenspan, CEO of the award-winning Sappington International Farmers Market. "Do not keep negative people around you. It zaps your energy."

It's also important to learn to trust your own instincts. I refer to it as "Go with your gut." Women have great instincts, and in the majority of situations if your gut is telling you it's a bad deal, it's a bad deal. Just think about how many times you've had a bad feeling about something and it turned out you were right. Hindsight is 20/20, but your instincts can give you a sneak preview.

So listen to your instincts. If something doesn't hit you just right, move on. Don't press the issue. Don't ever be afraid to walk away from a bad situation. As you are building your company, you want to establish trust and a safe environment for yourself, your employees, and your customers. Establishing yourself as a credible, authentic person with integrity and principles inspires confidence in your abilities as a true leader.

Cherish Yourself

Because the stress of growing your business can take its toll, it's important to take care of yourself to keep the passion alive and protect your business interests. Stress is the number one cause of illness in our country. Learning how to manage your stress level is not only a personally smart decision, but it's critical for managing your business. When you are stressed or not feeling well, your motivation level drops. Chances are your judgment will be impaired and you won't make good decisions. Your emotions easily rise to the surface, which can result in irrational displays of behavior.

Be realistic about what you expect of yourself and don't over commit. Learn to say "no" and really mean it. There are only so many hours in a day, and no matter how you try you can't change that. You need to manage your time and plan ahead so you can include time to focus on your well-being. If you don't, you'll burn out, and so will your business.

Try scheduling at least 15 minutes a day just for you. Put it on your calendar so nothing gets in the way. One woman told me she leaves her office once a week to take a piano lesson. It forces her to think about something entirely different for an hour, and she comes back feeling more refreshed.

Personally, I cook. It's a creative outlet for me and it takes my mind off of work. There are many evenings, when after a long stressful day, I'll come home and prepare a wonderful meal. When my husband and I were first married he didn't understand why I'd want to do that. He thought I'd prefer to go out to dinner. Now he gets it and enjoys the fruits of my labor.

"When I first stared the business, I worked all the time, seven days a week, nearly 24 hours a day. I really didn't take a break for about the first three years. I nearly wore myself out. Now, I plan for time off in advance, and I take time to take care of me. I have to schedule it, because it is real easy to get into that working-all-the-time routine. I don't think that is healthy for the long term, so I really try to make time for my family and myself," says Valerie Freeman, CEO and founder of Imprimis Group.

A good suggestion comes from Elizabeth Kearney, CEO of the California-based Kearney & Associates: The Experts Alliance, who says to make sure you calendar everything—particularly your personal time. "I just decide what amount of time I am going to need, and I actually put it on my calendar. Now that may sound stupid, but I write it down. Here's the time for my children. Here's time for this. I flex it if I need to, but if I don't put it down I won't even get to a party that I am planning on attending," she explains.

A Make Mine a $Million Business award winner, Julie Fogg, CEO of Active Port, a full-service reseller of Nortel converged telephone systems, says she has learned how important it is to keep her health and happiness as her two top priorities and her company will thrive as a result. She signed up for a fitness boot camp five days a week starting at 5:30 A.M. and sees a nutritionist regularly. "I have so much more energy now that I am careful about what I eat and I participate in group exercise. My health was affecting Active Port, so I will never neglect that area of my life again." Fogg goes on to recommend: "Read the *E-Myth Revisited* as many times as it takes for the information to sink in and take time away from the business both on weekends and during vacation time, regularly."

At Two Men and a Truck, working more than forty hours a week is not seen as a badge of honor. Says Melanie Bergeron:

> If you are staying late, we have a problem with your work flow, and that's not right. Or you are here because you want to be working those long hours. And we don't want that, either. Go home, be with your family. If you are content at home, you are going to be content at work. And if you are managing your time correctly you are going to do a better job for the forty hours you are here than if you are here for sixty.

Scheduling time for a regular exercise program and time off for personal enjoyment should be a priority. Of course, if you travel a lot, scheduling that time becomes even more difficult One of the things I have found that helps me when I'm on the road is a product called Travelsenthics. Basically, it's a deck of cards with various exercises on each card. You shuffle the cards and go through the entire deck in about twenty minutes. You'll be amazed. The product was invented by a former professional athlete who found it difficult to get adequate workouts on the road.

Most hotels today have fitness facilities, and you can always take your tennis shoes and go for a brisk walk. Even if you only walk for ten or twenty minutes, it's enough time to get your blood pumping and clear your mind.

Finally, I am going to sound like your mother here, but make sure you eat healthy. In fact, make sure you take time to eat, period. Are you like me—one of those people who skips meals or crams something in on the run or while working at the desk? Small meals several times a day will keep your energy up, your brain power working, and your weight under control.

Your body is your temple, so cherish it and take care of it. Without your health, your dreams of building a million dollar business won't come true.

Pay Yourself What You Are Worth

Originally, my partners and I self-funded SBTV.com, so for the first couple of years as we were getting the business off the ground, I joked that I loved my job so much I paid to go to work every day. Revenue that came into the business was used to build business operations, and so none of us took a salary.

Our situation isn't uncommon. Most startups don't have enough cash to pay the owners for a period of time, but your company's ability to pay a fair market salary to you is the sign of a healthy, viable enterprise. The first month SBTV.com became cash flow positive, I felt like a proud mom. During a meeting with one of our consultants, I bragged about how well our company was doing financially. The consultant responded by asking, "Yes, but are you paying yourself a fair market rate?"

Whoops. Missed that one on the test. My partners and I realized we needed to start paying ourselves a fair market salary, and our business needed to be strong enough to absorb that expense.

I believe this situation is often exacerbated with women business owners. Women have a tendency to undervalue themselves—both personally and in the pricing of their products and services. That's something you need to correct when you are building a million-dollar enterprise. If you are not being fairly rewarded for your efforts, you will more easily get disheartened, disillusioned, and burned out. As shoe designer and manufacturer Taryn Rose says:

When you are growing very fast, that's often the time when you have very little cash left for yourself, but I tell people, pay yourself first because you're always going to think you can sacrifice and sacrifice. At some point you need to change that attitude, and there is nothing wrong with making a lot of money. You've earned it. I think it's a good score card for how well you are playing the game.

Among members of the Women Presidents' Organization (WPO), there is no glass ceiling when it comes to compensation as CEOs of their million-dollar-plus companies. More than half of respondents to a Labor Day survey said they believe their salary is the same as their male counterparts, and over half said they plan to increase their salary and/or their bonus, benefits, commissions, partnership distributions, or compensation.

Says Marsha Firestone, the organization's founder and president, "Not only does our survey indicate that the glass ceiling has been shattered in the eyes of many women presidents, but also that the equality that entrepreneurship affords was a motivating factor for many to start their own businesses."

With fair compensation in mind, the WPO created the Mary Lehman MacLachlan Award for Entrepreneurial Excellence. Mary Lehman MacLachlan was an esteemed WPO advisory board member and a leader in the women's business community. She believed in the importance of women becoming economically independent. As Mary stated, "I really care about women in positions of leadership and ownership. Now is the time for women to claim their rightful place as capitalists in the greatest capitalist country in the world. And, in this effort, women need to support other women, because if they don't, no one else will."

The criteria for the award include sharing Mary's beliefs about economic independence and fairly compensating yourself as the business-owner. Additionally, the business must have positive financial benefits for its staff, including a competitive benefits package, strong training opportunities,and a program to give back to the community.

Don't undervalue your contribution to your business and its success. Pay yourself what you are worth. You deserve it.

Be an Unintentional Mentor

You may not realize it, but as a successful woman business owner, every day you set an example for others. Every day and in everything you do, you are leading by example, and so you must lead with character and integrity. The next generation is looking to you to learn how to do what you have done. Think about how you can reach back and help others. According to WBENC's founding architect Susan Bari:

> I think we are at a wonderful time in the history of America, and it's a wonderful time to be a woman business owner. We have looked at women business owners in other parts of the world, and we have been working with mentoring them and their organizations, but what we have seen here in the United States because of the efforts of women of my generation, we have really created a path that can be followed by the women of today. And they are creating their own roadways for their daughters and for the women business owners that are to come.

Interestingly, because of your success you never really know who is watching and emulating you. In fact, I think a lot of us would be surprised at just how many people look up to us as role models. You may not think of yourself as anyone special, but you really are.

Last spring, a young lady called me wanting some advice about a career decision. Because she was a casual acquaintance, I was a little surprised she chose me, but I was happy to help her think through the situation. Later, she was telling someone about how much I had helped her and she said, "Susan is my mentor." I have to admit it made me smile.

Throughout this book I have mentioned some of the great women who have truly been trailblazers and pioneers. I imagine most of these women would be surprised to learn about their legendary status, but it's true. I have often heard them referred to as celebrities because of all they have done. As you become a successful, million-dollar woman business owner, others will look up to you. Use your power wisely and for the good of the next generation of amazing women.

Choose Your Battles Wisely

Growing a business is fraught with challenges. There are times when you feel as though you want to tear your hair out. There are moments of frustration, anger, hurt, and disappointment. When things really seem out of control it's human nature to want to strike back, but in order to survive this wild roller-coaster ride, I strongly recommend you learn to choose your battles wisely.

As I have mentioned, travel is a business necessity for me. Our headquarters are in St. Louis, but I spend a significant amount of time in New York City and San Francisco. In addition, there are meetings and conferences all over the country, so I am on the road about half of my time, which is tiring and trying.

A little less than a year after Hurricane Katrina devastated the Gulf Coast, I was asked to speak at a conference for women business owners in Biloxi, Mississippi. I flew from the National Women Business Owners annual conference in San Francisco to Biloxi, stopping in Dallas to change planes. The plane to Biloxi was a small, regional jet liner. We were held up on the runway for quite some time and the pilot explained there were concerns about the weight of the aircraft. Finally, we took off. I made it to Biloxi but my luggage didn't.

I walked over to the ticket counter and waited for someone to arrive. A nice young man began to address those of us who were looking for answers. I learned my bag had been taken off the plane in

Dallas to reduce the weight of the aircraft. My bag—the one marked with "Premium Service" and "Platinum Status."

"Okay, when does the next flight arrive?" I asked.

"Tomorrow morning at 10:45," the agent said.

Okay, now we had a problem. My keynote address was scheduled for 9:00 a.m. the next day. The young man apologized a million times, but there really wasn't anything he could do. Plus, he had nothing to do with the decision that was made back in Dallas.

So there I stood in my flip-flops and casual black slacks, having traveled all day, and knowing I had nothing to wear for my speech in the morning. It was decision time. Normally I am a stickler for customer service, and I would have been pretty angry at the lack of service this airline had provided, but the employees at the Biloxi airport were powerless, and getting angry at them would accomplish nothing except upsetting me. I chose to accept the situation and make the best of it.

I purchased personal care items in the gift shop, along with a t-shirt to sleep in and a clean rhinestone studded t-shirt that spelled Biloxi to wear the next day. I washed my under garments in the sink and focused on my presentation.

As I stood before the audience the next day, I used this situation to illustrate the importance of recognizing the times in our lives when we can't control the situation and we have to let it go. Afterwards, some of the women in the audience said they thought I was starting a new trend with the flip-flops. So there you have it.

Choosing your battles wisely can also keep you from unnecessarily burning bridges. There are times in business when you have to close the door on a relationship, whether it's a customer, supplier, or even an employee, but those situations are few and far between. In most cases, the wiser course of action is to take the high road, resolve the situation to the best of your ability, and move on.

A few years ago, I was working on a special project and I asked a friend of mine whether she knew any good freelance writers who would be interested in picking up some extra work. She said her company—a public relations firm—was going through a slow period and she'd be happy to take on the project. We agreed on the scope of the work and a fee. Unfortunately, our agreement was very informal—just a couple of e-mails. It was unfortunate, because she failed miserably. She didn't come close to doing the scope of the work I needed, and much of what she did provide wasn't useable. Nonetheless, she sent an invoice for the full amount. Honestly, I was shocked, but I thought we could work out a settlement that would be fair to both of us. I calculated an amount based on the percentage of the work she completed, including what wasn't useable, and offered to pay her based on that. I heard nothing from her until almost a year later when she sued me for copyright infringement. You see, because she didn't have anything in writing to support a contract, her artful attorney found another avenue to attack.

To make a long story short, I paid the full amount, but talk about being short-sighted on her part. She burned a bridge that can never be repaired. She has a public relations firm, and I am in the media business. Now, do you think any of her clients will ever get coverage on my network? I'll let you figure that out for yourself.

So be careful and weigh each situation carefully. Ask yourself what are the long-term consequences of my actions? Is it worth burning a bridge that may have value in the future?

Business battles can zap your energy and detract you from your priorities. You don't want to waste your intellect and energy on negative situations you can't control. Choose your battles wisely.

Expect the Unexpected

It often takes a disaster of great magnitude to remind us how vulnerable we are. After 9/11, not only did we mourn the loss of so many innocent lives, but we also witnessed the tremendous impact on small business. Thousands of small companies were literally wiped out that fateful day. Many never recovered.

As a result of the 9/11 devastation, small firms recognized the need to be prepared for the unexpected. Disaster preparedness became a hot topic, forcing small business owners to focus on what steps they needed to take in order to minimize the impact of a disaster on their business. But as time passed, memories faded, and the sense of urgency diminished.

Enter Hurricanes Rita and Katrina. Once again, many small firms suffered major losses due to the fury of these hurricanes. Almost overnight, many entrepreneurs who had spent years building their businesses watched helplessly as the storm wiped them out.

According to a survey conducted in 2004 by the National Federation of Independent Business, 30 percent of operating small businesses have been closed 24 hours or longer because of a natural disaster. Of the respondents who had experienced a disaster, 62 percent said the biggest problem was the loss of sales and customers; 18 percent said that the biggest problem was uninsured losses. Think about it from this perspective. If you were faced with a disaster and you had only five minutes to grab the essentials to maintain operations, what would you do? What would you grab?

In order to protect your business, your employees, and your customers, you should take the time to create a business continuity plan, and do so sooner rather than later. Your plan should address employee safety and data protection. You should make a list of business essentials required to keep your business up and running. Don't forget to keep emergency supplies on hand, such as water, food, a first-aid kit, and a battery-operated radio with extra batteries. You might want to consider purchasing an auxiliary generator to keep your power on during emergencies.

Make sure you examine your insurance coverage. Meet with your insurance provider to review your current coverage for such things as physical losses, flood coverage, and business interruption. Think about how you'll pay creditors and employees and how you will provide for your own income if your business is interrupted.

Crisis situations aren't always related to natural disasters or terrorist/criminal attacks. What if one of your key employees walks out the door without notice, or becomes critically ill? Do you have a contingency plan, or will such a situation jeopardize your business? When you have a small staff, the loss of an employee who is integral to your business operations can create such a void that you may not be able to overcome it for quite some time. Do yourself a favor and explore your options now. Identify and verify options in advance.

As I am writing this book, my partner Michael is fighting a rare and aggressive cancer. I can't begin to explain how upsetting it is both personally and professionally. Michael is an integral part of SBTV.com's success. Even though we thought we'd never need it, a couple of years ago we created a business contingency plan. For his responsibilities, we identified two individuals who could step into his shoes if, as he said, "I get hit by a bus." This foresight has been a lifesaver for the business. As difficult and painful as these types of situations can be, you must force yourself to discuss them openly and have a written plan, and then hope you never have to use it.

All in all, it really doesn't matter what type of crisis you face, what is most important is how well and how fast you are able to respond to it. No matter what type of business you are in or where you are located, there are going to be setbacks. You can't predict the future, but you can be prepared for it.

Reap the Ultimate Reward: Giving Back

Successful women entrepreneurs are rewarded by the fact that they can make a difference by giving back. Some assist their employees and their families by helping children go through college or by providing assistance during a serious family illness. Others are active in their community or with charitable organizations. Some get involved in political advocacy. There is strong evidence that women entrepreneurs view philanthropy as a top priority.

Earlier in the chapter I mentioned the devastation of Hurricanes Katrina and Rita. Immediately following those disasters, a number of women's business organizations stepped up to the plate to come to the aid of their sisters in the Gulf Coast Region. NAWBO raised $40,000 in forty-five days, all from contributions from women business owners. The organization distributed the funds to sixteen women business owners via direct grants. "We received a lot of thanks from those who got the grants, as our funds were some of the first they received because insurance and federal aid were so tied up," says Executive Director Erin Fuller.

Denise Dussom is one woman business owner who received a grant and was virtually adopted by the Dallas/Ft. Worth NAWBO Chapter. "She and her business partner moved to that area to live with family, since her home and business were destroyed. NAWBO members helped find her equipment, clothing, and business opportunities to get up and running in a new town," Erin said.

Other organizations launched fundraising initiatives, as well. WBENC raised another $40,000 for certified women business enterprises.

It's common for business owners to make charitable contributions through their businesses, and many have programs to encourage their employees to volunteer. Women business owners tend to be more motivated toward philanthropic endeavors than their male counterparts. Ninety-two percent of women, as compared to 88 percent of men, contribute money to charities, according to the Center for Women's Business Research. In fact, about one-third of women business owners make significant personal charitable contributions of $5,000 a year or more.

"We actually found in our study that women were more likely than men to write the checks over $1,000 dollars, which surprised the whole world," says Sharon Hadary, executive director of the Center.

Sharon also notes that in addition to writing checks, women are more likely to get involved in the organizations they support. Fully half (52 percent) of women business owners state that their level of financial support has recently increased, and 51 percent say that the hours devoted to charitable activities have likewise increased. Sharon adds:

> These women not only lead their businesses, they are leading charitable organizations by serving on boards, and chairing fundraisers and special events. High net-worth women business owners are even more philanthropic than their male counterparts. Half (50 percent) of women with assets of $1 million or more contribute at least $10,000 annually to charity, compared to 40 percent of men entrepreneurs. While women and men business owners with high net worth both volunteer an average of about 16 hours a month, 94 percent of these women, compared to 83 percent of the men, serve in leadership positions with charitable organizations.

Barbara Kasoff and Terry Neese are both successful women entrepreneurs, and both have been deeply involved in politics for many years. Although on opposite sides of the aisle, the two came together to create a not-for-profit organization—Women Impacting Public Policy, or WIPP. As a national bipartisan public policy organization, WIPP advocates for and on behalf of women and minorities in business, strengthening their sphere of influence in the legislative process of our nation, creating economic opportunities, and building bridges and alliances to other small business organizations. Today, WIPP's membership base exceeds 500,000. Building the organization has been a labor of love for Kasoff and Neese. As Kasoff explains:

> Even though women have made great strides over the years and are recognized by many as the engine that fuels our economy, there is a distinct feeling that something is missing. I

strongly believe that it is the ability for us to leverage our power politically and proactively address the critical issues that affect us as business owners.

Giving back is important to Adesso founder Peggy Traub: "I feel I have been blessed with both good health, a great spouse, and a financially successful company, so I am very focused on charity. For example, my spouse and I award three annual scholarships to college students. Also, I'm a member of the Women's Leadership Board at the Kennedy School at Harvard. Last year, I created a Fellowship for the KSG students to do research on a topic concerning gay issues and public policy. In 2006 our Fellow spent the summer in Brazil researching the impact of government policies on the spread of AIDS in that country. And at Adesso, we donate thousands of dollars of free products annually." She adds, "Giving back to others helps bring meaning and satisfaction to me both personally and professionally."

"People tell us we should put money in a foundation and just support one organization. My mom likes spreading the goodwill. Our accountant friends tell us it's not helping us tax wise to give away this much money. But that's not why we do it. We do it because it makes us feel good, and I think that's because we came from nothing. We can afford it, so we do it. If we can't afford it, we'll just start cutting back a little bit," explains Melanie Bergeron.

Patty DeDominic is the founder and CEO of PDQ Careers Group of companies, one of Los Angeles' largest privately held staffing services. In 2006, she pledged a $1 million challenge grant to the Los Angeles chapter of the National Association of Women Business Owners, and its educational nonprofit, the Enterprise Institute of NAWBO-LA. It is the largest gift from a single business owner ever received by a local chapter or the national organization. The gift is a matching grant, with the chapter having ten years to raise an identical amount from individual donors.

"NAWBO has for decades been close to my heart, and it helped me in my own business success," Patty says. "There are many alternatives when it comes to giving, but I wanted to ensure NAWBO's valuable work would continue and that other entrepreneurs would be similarly inspired to contribute."[1]

Similarly, Patty gave a $100,000 matching gift to help launch the Foundation for SCORE. That gift resulted in contributions from more than 900 individuals, exceeding the original grant amount.

Recently, Decor & You launched its Charitable Foundation. According to cofounder Karen Powell, her dog Mitch, who was sort of the office dog, passed away two years earlier from a rare blood disease. In response, her staff created "Hug Your Pet Day," which is November 20.

"I had some bookmarks made up for Hug Your Pet Day and I started handing them out. Then it occurred to me that someone else would pick up the idea and make money on it. If anybody was going to make money I wanted it to be a charitable foundation," Powell says. At their annual conference, the company launched the Decor & You Charitable Foundation and raised $5,500 for Katrina Relief and Noah's Ark for pet relief. Each year, they plan to select two different charities as beneficiaries.

Building a million-dollar business not only provides economic stability for you, your family, and your employees, but it also creates the opportunity for you to truly make a difference in this world.

You Can Do It

At this point, I hope you are inspired and have the confidence to go for the gold—to spread your wings and set a goal of growing your business to a million-dollar enterprise and beyond. Dream your dream. State your intention. Plan your strategy. Before you know it your dream will be a reality.

Running a business will never be easy. If it were easy, everyone would do it, but if you are committed, determined, passionate, patient, and persevering, I am confident you have what it takes to be a million-dollar woman business owner. I am anxious to hear about your success. Trust me. If I can do it, you can do it. Good luck. Here's to your million-dollar business! You look like a million to me.

10

GREAT RESOURCES

The challenge of writing a book like this one is getting to the point where you feel as though it's complete. There is so much to cover and so much to say. It's almost like the never-ending story. However, it's humanly impossible to address everything, and even if I could you'd never have time to read it all. Therefore, I want to leave you with some great resources that I believe can help you accelerate your business growth. This list is not all-encompassing by any means, but these are some of my favorites. I hope you'll find them useful, too.

Association of Women's Business Centers
The Association of Women's Business Centers (AWBC) develops and strengthens a global network of women's business centers to advance the growth and success of women business owners. The vision of

AWBC is a world where economic justice, wealth, and well-being are realized through the collective leadership and power of successful entrepreneurial women. www.awbc.biz

Athena Foundation

The Athena Foundation pairs woman-owned businesses with a group of local mentors who serve as a panel of advisors. Advisors work with the business owner on her business for one year at no charge. www.AthenaFoundation.org

Business Women's Network

The Business Women's Network is a membership organization dedicated to promoting women in all aspects of business. BWN provides resources and contacts to help women succeed. www.bwni.com

Center for Women's Business Research

The Center for Women's Business Research, founded as the National Foundation of Women Business Owners, provides original, groundbreaking research to document the economic and social contributions of women-owned firms and consulting and public relation services to maximize the benefits of that knowledge. www.cfwbr.org

Count Me In

Count Me In champions the cause for women's economic independence by providing access to business loans, consultation, and education. The first online microlender, Count Me In uses a unique, women-friendly credit scoring system to make loans of $500 to $10,000 available to women across the United States who have nowhere to turn for that all-important first business loan. The organization provides access to networks that expand contacts, markets, skills, and confidence. www.countmein.org

Direct Selling Association

The Direct Selling Association (DSA) is the national trade association of the leading firms that manufacture and distribute goods and services sold directly to consumers. More than 200 companies are members of the association, including many well-known brand names. The DSA's mission is "To protect, serve and promote the effectiveness of member companies and the independent business people they represent. To ensure that the marketing by member companies of products and/or the direct sales opportunity is conducted with the highest level of business ethics and service to consumers." www.dsa.org

Golden Seeds

Golden Seeds plays an instrumental role in supporting women to utilize both their intrinsic and financial capital to its full potential. It identifies and invests in women-led ventures with the potential to grow into multimillion-dollar businesses while enabling accredited investors to invest alongside Golden Seeds. It provides entrepreneurs with strategic business advice as well as access to funding and the tools to enable them to grow into multimillion-dollar businesses. www.goldenseeds.com

International Franchise Association

The International Franchise Association (IFA), the oldest and largest franchising trade group, strives to educate prospective franchise investors so that they are fully equipped to handle the challenges of becoming small-business entrepreneurs. IFA serves more than 1,200 franchisor, 8,000 franchisee, and 400 supplier members. Its mission is to safeguard the business environment for franchising worldwide. www.franchise.org

Ladies Who Launch

Ladies Who Launch provides content and community to help women start and expand their businesses and creative ventures. Through their events, e-mail newsletter, website, and in-person incubator programs, Ladies Who Launch provides a venue for motivated women to exchange products and services, ideas, and strategic relationships. Ladies Who Launch connects thousands of women to each other by giving them multiple forums in which to connect and ultimately propel their entrepreneurial visions forward in ways they may never have dreamed possible. www.ladieswholaunch.com

Make Mine a $Million Business

Make Mine a $Million Business is a program of Count Me In for Women's Economic Independence, and of founding partner, OPEN, from American Express. The program provides a combination of money, mentoring, marketing, and technology tools that women entrepreneurs need to help grow their businesses from micro to millions. www.makemineamillion.org

Mom Inventors

Mom Inventors, Inc.'s mission is to develop, manufacture, and sell quality Mom Invented™ branded products throughout the United States and Europe; to help inventors take their products from concept to market by providing a highly informative, interactive community-based website and offering the best inventor-education services in the field; and to highlight and publicize the historical and present-day inventive contributions of moms by both licensing products invented by moms and publicly crediting them for their inventions. www.mominventors.com

National Association for the Self-Employed

The National Association for the Self-Employed (NASE) is the nation's leading resource for the self-employed and micro-businesses providing a broad range of benefits and support to help the smallest businesses succeed. www.nase.org

National Association of Women Business Owners

The National Association of Women Business Owners (NAWBO) is the voice of America's 10.6 million women-owned businesses. Since 1975, NAWBO has helped women evolve their businesses by sharing resources and providing a single voice to shape economic and public policy. NAWBO is the only dues-based national organization representing the interests of all women entrepreneurs across all industries. www.nawbo.org

National Federation of Independent Businesses

The National Federation of Independent Businesses (NFIB) is the leading advocacy organization representing small and independent businesses. A nonprofit, nonpartisan organization founded in 1943, NFIB represents the consensus views of its members in Washington and all fifty state capitals. NFIB's mission is to promote and protect the right of its members to own, operate, and grow their businesses. NFIB also gives its members a power in the marketplace. www.nfib.org

National Minority Supplier Development Council

Providing a direct link between corporate America and minority-owned businesses is the primary objective of the National Minority Supplier Development Council (NMSDC), one of the country's leading business membership organizations. There are 3,500 corporate members throughout the network, including most of America's largest publicly-owned, privately-owned, and foreign-owned companies, as well as universities, hospitals, and other buying institutions. The regional councils certify and match more than 15,000 minority-owned businesses (Asian, Black, Hispanic, and Native American) with member corporations that want to purchase goods and services. www.nmsdc.org

National Women's Business Council

The National Women's Business Council (NWBC) is a bipartisan federal advisory council created to serve as an independent source of advice and policy recommendations to the president, Congress, and the U.S. Small Business Administration on economic issues of importance to women business owners. The Council's mission is to promote bold initiatives, policies, and programs designed to support women's business enterprises at all stages of development in the public and private sector marketplaces—from startup to success to significance. www.nwbc.gov

SBA's Online Women's Business Center

Office of Women's Business Ownership's Online Women's Business Center helps women achieve their dreams and improve their communities by helping them start and run successful businesses, regardless of social or financial disadvantage, race, ethnicity, or business background. www.onlinewbc.gov

SCORE—Counselors to America's Small Business

SCORE—Counselors to America's Small Business is America's premier source of free and confidential small business advice for entrepreneurs. SCORE's 10,500 volunteer counselors have more than 600 business skills. Volunteers are working or retired business owners, executives, and corporate leaders who share their wisdom and lessons learned in business. www.score.org

Small Business Development Centers

Small Business Development Centers (SBDCs) provide management assistance to current and prospective small-business owners. They offer one-stop assistance to individuals and small businesses by providing a wide variety of information and guidance in central and easily accessible branch locations. www.sba.gov/sbdc

Springboard Enterprises

Springboard Enterprises is a national nonprofit organization accelerating women's access to the equity markets. Its programs educate, showcase, and support women entrepreneurs as they seek equity capital and to grow their companies. www.springboardenterprises.com

U.S. Small Business Administration

The U.S. Small Business Administration (SBA) was created in 1953 as an independent agency of the federal government to aid, counsel, assist, and protect the interests of small business concerns, to preserve free competitive enterprise, and to maintain and strengthen the over-all economy of our nation. The SBA helps Americans start, build, and grow businesses. Through an extensive network of field offices and partnerships with public and private organizations, SBA delivers its services to people throughout the United States, Puerto Rico, the U. S. Virgin Islands and Guam. www.sba.gov

Women Impacting Public Policy

The voice for women in business in our nation's capital, Women Impacting Public Policy, Inc. (WIPP) is a national bipartisan public policy organization that advocates for and on behalf of women and minorities in business, strengthening their sphere of influence in the legislative process of our nation, creating economic opportunities, and building bridges and alliances to other small business organizations. Through WIPP, our collective voice makes a powerful impact on Capitol Hill and with the administration. www.wipp.org

Women Presidents' Organization

The Women Presidents' Organization (WPO) locally and internationally connects top women entrepreneurs at the million- and multimillion-dollar level ($2 million in gross annual sales or $1 million for service-based business) for greater personal and professional success. In monthly meetings across the United States and Canada, chapters composed of twenty accomplished women presidents from diverse industries and backgrounds invest time and energy in themselves and their businesses to drive their corporations to the next level. www.womenpresidentsorg.com

Women's Business Enterprise National Council

The Women's Business Enterprise National Council (WBENC), founded in 1997, is the nation's leading advocate of women-owned businesses as suppliers to America's corporations. It also is the largest third-party certifier of businesses owned and operated by women in the United States. WBENC works to foster diversity in the world of commerce with programs and policies designed to expand opportunities and eliminate barriers in the marketplace for women business owners. WBENC works with representatives of corporations to encourage the utilization and expansion of supplier/vendor diversity programs. www.wbenc.org

Women's Technology Cluster

The Women's Technology Cluster (WTC) is the preeminent business incubator in the United States dedicated to women leaders building technology-driven businesses. Its mission is to increase the number of successful companies and to leverage their influence. Through a dedicated community of proven CEOs, investors, and industry experts, the WTC provides extensive advisory services, coaching, and access to business and capital networks. www.wtc-sf.org

APPENDIX

Celebrating our Successes

Small business is the economic backbone of the United States. Small businesses employ nearly two-thirds of the entire U.S. workforce. These firms spend $4.7 trillion annually on non-payroll expenses and represent 50 percent of the GDP in this country. So with women opening firms at twice the rate of their male counterparts, it's no wonder they are drawing a lot of attention. But is all the hoopla because women business ownership is a new trend or fad?

Women-owned and women-led firms are not a new phenomenon. The United States was built on the foundation of small business. Our country really has come full circle in many ways. We started as a land of entrepreneurs, progressed through the industrial age to the information age, and we now have returned to the age of the entrepreneur.

Many of the businesses in the Colonial era were owned and/or operated by women. Baker Library at Harvard University owns a collection of accounts of female-owned businesses from the eighteenth and nineteenth centuries. These papers document women-owned taverns, general stores, millinery shops, schools, farms, cider mills, and saw mills. In 1718, a law was passed in Pennsylvania extending independent trader status to "wives of mariners and others, whose circumstances as well as vocations oblige them to go to sea." The Declaration of Independence was printed by the only printer in Baltimore in 1777, Katherine Mary Goddard.

An accurate account of early women-owned firms is problematic because the law didn't recognize women as separate legal entities. Under early colonial law, married women had no right to enter into contracts, inherit property, sue, or be sued. Society believed women needed to be protected.

"Our ladies know nothing of the sober certainties which related to money and they cannot be taught," wrote Frederic Tudor in 1820, in an indictment of women's financial abilities that was typical of the period.

Abigail Adams, the beloved wife of the second president of the United States, was actually quite the business woman. Her skill at managing the family farm and running other business affairs freed her husband's time so he could devote himself to public service. (Sounds familiar, doesn't it?) While John was serving in Congress, she wrote to him and said, "Remember the ladies and be more generous and favorable to them than your ancestors. If particular care is not paid to the Ladies we are determined to form a rebellion, and will not hold ourselves bound by any Laws in which we have no voice or Representation."

Her loving husband, John, replied in a letter dated April 14, 1776, "As to your extraordinary code of laws, I cannot but laugh."

In 1809, Mary Dixon Kies, received the first patent ever given to a woman for weaving straw and thread for millinery making. Sarah E. Goode became the first African-American woman to receive a patent for a bed that folded up into a cabinet.

In 1885, Susan Taylor Converse's one-piece flannel Emancipation Suit eliminated the need for a suffocating corset and became an immediate success. There was an outcry by many women's groups for Converse to forgo her royalty on each garment sold, but she refused. "With all your zeal for women's rights, how could you even suggest that one woman like myself should give of her head and hand labor without fair compensation?" she responded.

Some women inherited their businesses, but others, like women today, used their own initiative and finances to launch their enterprises. The first self-made female millionaire in American history was born to former slaves in 1867. Madam C.J. Walker, said, "I got my start by giving myself a start."

During the 1890s, Walker lost most of her hair because of a scalp ailment. After experimenting with many homemade remedies and store bought products, she created a treatment that helped her hair grow. Subsequently, she started her own company selling Madam Walker's Wonderful Hair Grower, which she claimed had been revealed to her in a dream. She traveled for more than a year throughout the South and Southeast promoting her products and selling them door to door. Ultimately, she moved to Indianapolis where she built a factory, a hair and manicure salon, and a training school. As her business grew, she organized agents into local and state clubs. Many believe her Madam C.J. Walker Hair Culturists Union of America convention in Philadelphia in 1917 must have been one of the first national meetings of businesswomen in the country.

"Walker encouraged other Black women to leave unpromising careers as poorly paid washerwomen and maids to become Walker Agents and earn commission," said Erica Littlejohn Burnette, cofounder and vice president of marketing for Our Own Image. Headquartered in Ohio, her company offers African-American party supplies, gift bags, keepsakes, journals,and home accessories.[1]

The Industrial Revolution brought important changes in laws affecting women in business. Slowly, the states began to pass legislation which allowed women to own property, enter into contracts and borrow money. Of course, even though women could legally borrow funds, the banks remained largely uninterested because society continued to frown on the notion of women owning their own business.

At the end of the nineteenth century, as women were fighting for the right to vote, they were also speaking out for economic equality. In 1895, Irene Hardy—whom one might call the early version of Suze Orman—wrote *How to Make Money Although a Woman.* By today's standards it would probably be a bestseller.

Women entering the workforce in World War II (and the strong support of small business in general) helped improve the acceptance and recognition of women entrepreneurs. My mother was a post-World War II business owner. After the war, she and her brother opened a furniture store in a small southern Missouri town. When she married my father, she sold her interest in that business and opened a retail clothing store. In 1963, she and my father became business partners in a funeral home business. Growing up with a mother who was a business owner seemed normal to me, but looking back on her life, I imagine people saw her as an oddity—a female entrepreneur in a small town. I imagine it couldn't have been easy for her.

The passage of the 1974 Equal Credit Opportunity Act is often cited as one of the most important factors in the growth of women-owned business. With the passage of the act, married women were guaranteed the right to obtain credit in their own names, making it easier for women business owners to gain access to capital. In 1988, Congress passed the Women's Business Ownership Act, which amended the Credit Opportunity Act to include business loans and prohibit lenders from inquiring about marital status or a spouse's occupation. The act also provided training and assistance to women business owners and led to the formation of Women's Business Centers. It expanded the census data collected on women-owned businesses to include those that are 51 percent women-owned.

The law may have been on the books, but it had little impact. Women found getting a business loan in their own right was nearly impossible. There are countless stories of successful women entrepreneurs who had to take their husbands along in order to get a line of credit for their business.

Bonny Filandrinos, president of Staffing Solutions, was running her business for three years, with a track record of profitability, when she decided to get a line of credit. She went to four banks who gave her ridiculous and insulting terms before she found one that would look at her track record instead of her marital status.

Imprimis CEO Valerie Freeman says credibility was a serious problem. "It was so difficult to get a line of credit from any financial institution. In fact, in the beginning I had to have my accountant go with me on a call to a financial institution to get my initial line of credit," she remembers.

Pizza entrepreneur Patty Phillips recalls her first experience trying to get a bank loan as a disheartening experience, as well. She went to seven banks and says the last loan officer basically told her all she would have to do is get married, get pregnant, and quit the business. "I was so shocked and disgusted, I just walked away. It was too much of a waste of time to worry about someone who thinks that way," she says.

These stories may seem as though they are in the distant past, but I bet there are a number of you who don't think of the 1970s and 1980s as ancient history. I certainly don't.

The Omnibus Women's Ownership Act of 1991 created the National Women's Business Council to promote business women's access to contracts, purchase orders, credit, statistics, and managerial and technical assistance. Then in 1993, the 103rd U.S. Congress passed two important initiatives providing expanded opportunities for women business owners:

> ➤ The Office of Women's Business Ownership was permanently established by legislation reauthorizing the Small Business Administration.

> ➤ The Federal Acquisitions Streamlining Act required federal agencies to establish a 5-percent procurement goal for women-owned businesses (a goal still not met).

Both of these provisions are found in the Women's Business Procurement Assistance Act, introduced as part of the Economic Equity Act.

So the concept of women as entrepreneurs is not a new phenomenon, trend, or fad. Rather, women business owners have always been a part of our country's economic history. What is new is the development of policies, changes in societal attitudes, and legal decisions that have begun to recognize, support, and liberate women as business owners.

You are in the right place at the right time. According to a 2007 forecast by the Institute for the Future, the face of small business will dramatically change. The research notes that the new entrepreneurs will be far more diverse than their predecessors in age, origin, and gender. By 2017, the white, middle-aged men who traditionally launch small businesses will be outnumbered by Generation Yers (those born after 1982), women, immigrants, and "un-retiring" baby boomers opting for entrepreneurship as a second career.

According to Ann Marie Almeida, president and CEO of the Association of Women's Business Centers:

> We continue to witness that women entrepreneurs offer society with answers and solutions to organization and business challenges and are well suited to leverage entrepreneurial opportunities. Women in enterprise are a solution to our economic and societal challenges and provide the tools to rebuild our civil society and our lives.[2]

The opportunities are there for you—to create an enterprise with meaning and purpose—to become economically independent—to favorably impact the lives of many. The road has been paved for you and now it's your turn.

NOTES

CHAPTER 1

1. Laurie Zuckerman, "Defeat Your Doubters: Your Worst Critic Is Often That Little Voice in Your Head," *My Business Magazine* online (www.nfib.com), February/March 2000.

2. Small Business Awards Program Book, *Small Business Week of Eastern Missouri*, 2005.

CHAPTER 2

1. Aliza P. Sherman, "Q&A with Lillian Vernon—An Entrepreneurial Icon," *Enterprising Women Magazine* online (www.enterprisingwomen.com), Winter 2005.

CHAPTER 3

1. Bureau of Labor Statistics, 2003.

2. Kay Koplovitz, "Human Capital Pays Dividends for Entrepreneurs," March 15, 2005. eVenturing, Kaurman Foundation website. Accessed August 11, 2006.

3. Center for Women's Business Research press release.

4. *Enterprising Women staff, Enterprising Women Magazine* 7, 4 (2006); online (www.enterprisingwomen.com).

CHAPTER 4

1. Steven S. Little, "The 7 Irrefutable Rules of Small Business Growth" (New York: John Wiley & Sons, 2005), p. 86.

2. "Talk of the Town," *Exchange: The Magazine for Entrepreneurial Women*, Premiere Issue, 2004, p. 32.

3. Helen Coster, "In This Together," *Forbes*, July 3, 2006, p. 80.

4. Kirstin Carey, *Out of the Mouths of Babes*, An Orange Tree Series Book (Philadelphia: Small Talk Marketing & Communications, Inc., 2004) p. 37.

CHAPTER 5

1. Judie Freeman, "Spotlight: Diane Buzzeo," *Enterprising Women Magazine* online (www.enterprisingwomen.com), Summer 2005.

2. Carol A. Hacker, *The Costs of Bad Hiring Decisions & How to Avoid Them*, 2nd edition (Boca Raton, Florida: Saint Lucie Press, 1998).

3. *Training New Employees*, SBTV.com, produced by Danita Blackwood, June 2004.

4. Rebecca Olson, "Hiring the Right People," *Enterpring Women Magazine* online (www.enterprisingwomen.com), Summer 2005.

5. Aliza P. Sherman, "Q&A with Lillian Vernon—An Entrepreneurial Icon," *Enterprising Women Magazine* online (www.enterprisingwomen.com), Summer 2005.

CHAPTER 6

1. Suzanne Vranica, "Small Firms Try Out New Advertising Avenues" *Startup Journal: The Wall Street Journal Center for Entrepreneurs* (www.startupjournal.com).

2. Suzanne B. Squyres, "WBENC Leader Eyes New Reality and Bigger Deals for WBE's," *WE: Women's Enterprise USA*, March/April 2006, p. 28.

CHAPTER 7

1. Julie Garella, "Are You a Lifestyle Maker or an Empire Builder?" *Enterprising Women Magazine* online (www.enterprisingwomen.com), Summer 2005.

2. "Women Business Owners' Access to Capital," Center for Women's Business Research press release, March 23, 2005.

3. Hannah Clark, "Are Angel Investors Heaven-Sent?" Forbes.com.

4. Garella, "Are You a Lifestyle Maker or an Empire Builder?"

5. Pascal N. Levensohn, "Rites of Passage: Managing CEO Transition in Venture-Backed Technology Companies," Levensohn Venture Partners White Paper, January 2006.

6. "Meet Julie Aigner-Clark, Featured Ladies on Ladies Who Launch." Available at: www.ladieswholaunch.com/featuredlady. Accessed September 3, 2006.

7. "Myth Buster: Women Entrepreneurs Prepare As Well As Men and Care More About Employees When Selling Business," Center for Women's Business Research, October 11, 2006.

CHAPTER 8

1. Women Business Enterprise National Council, *2005 Business Star* video, produced by SBTV Creative.

2. Center for Women's Business Research, "Access to Markets: Perspective from Large Corporations and Women's Business Enterprises." Commissioned by WBENC and the Ewing Marion Kauffman Foundation, 2003.

3. Sheryl Nance-Nash, "Going Global," *Priority* magazine, September 2006, p. 29.

4. "American Retail Tradition Rises to New Heights," press release from the Direct Selling Association, February 15, 2006.

5. Featured Mom Inventors: Silpada Designs," www.mominventors.com

APPENDIX

1. "Before Mary Kay and Tupperware, Madam C.J. Walker Went Knocking: DSA Honors Direct Selling Pioneers," DCA press release, August 19, 2006.

2. "AWBCbiz: The Voice of Women Business Owners and Women Entrepreneurs," Association of Women's Business Centers newsletter, Fall 2006, p. 2.

INDEX